# The Duty To Retreat

*A Review of the Evolution of the Duty to Retreat,
the Castle Doctrine, Florida's Stand Your Ground
Law and relevant Court Cases*

Jason C. King

ISBN-10: 1511939699
ISBN-13: 978-1511939630

# DEDICATION

I dedicate this book to my late Father, Stephen J. King. I miss our intellectual conversations we had about the world and politics. Thanks for encouraging me to finish law school. You are missed by all of us immensely.

A special thanks to my beautiful wife for her love and support. Thank you for teaching me the meaning of true love, unconditional love. I love you more today than yesterday, but not quite as much as I will tomorrow.

# ABOUT THE AUTHOR

Jason C. King was born in Lakeland, Florida in 1979 to Edith and Stephen King. His parents moved to southwest Florida when he was 12 years old. He graduated from Cypress Lake High School and went on to attend college at Edison State College (recently renamed Florida SouthWestern State College. He moved on to graduate with a bachelor's degree in Criminal Justice Administration in 2008 from the University of Phoenix. Jason then pursued his lifelong dream of attending law school and graduated from Ave Maria School of Law in 2012 with a doctorate in jurisprudence. Jason has been in the legal field for over fifteen years working as a paralegal and law clerk for law firms in various areas of the law including family law, real estate, general civil litigation, personal injury and criminal defense. Jason is not a member of the Florida Bar. Jason is married and he and his wife have a total of five children.

Jason C. King

# TABLE OF CONTENTS

# INTRODUCTION

*Se Defendendo*
The Evolution of the Duty to Retreat

The duty to retreat was born of English common law through the idea that all homicides are public wrongs and disputes between persons were to be resolved by the Crown. The doctrine imposed a duty to retreat upon a person being assaulted until he came "to the wall," and then, and only then, was he permitted to kill in self- defense. Such a defense was described as "homicide *se defendendo*."

It is understood that a difference of opinion existed among legal scholars as to the requirement of the duty retreat to the wall. While they agree as to the right of a man to defend himself if assaulted, they disagree on the requirement to retreat to the wall. A review of the writings of the legal scholars on the subject suggests that they were not all that different in their view of the duty to retreat and when it applied.

We will review the birth of the duty to retreat from English common law, its clarification by legal scholars, and its adoption in Florida until the enactment of the Stand Your Ground legislation in 2005.

# CHAPTER 1

# DEVELOPMENT OF
# THE DUTY TO RETREAT

## Sir Edward Coke

Sir Edward Coke (1552-1634), an early English jurist, Member of

Parliament and, in 1590, he became England's Attorney General under the

reign of Queen Elizabeth I. Coke is most notably known for authoring the

*Institutes of the Laws of England.*[1] Coke's work, deemed the first compilation of

law text book was brought to North America on the Mayflower and used in

the colonies. Therein Coke establishes the now know "Castle Doctrine"

wherein Coke states that "A man's house is his castle...and where shall a

---

[1] Humphry W. Woolrych, The Life of Sir Edward Coke, Knt. Lord Chief Justice of
the King's Bench (London: J.&W.T. Clarke, 1826)

man be safe if it be not in his own house?" This protected place included all places the person had the lawful right to be (Home, place of work, or guest in another's home).[2]

In addition, Coke set forth a man has the right to defend himself, including the use of deadly force, when attacked – *Se Defendendo*. Coke separated these types of homicide into two categories, justifiable and excusable. The former being performed in the execution of judgment and the latter being done for the protection of one's person or property. However, in some circumstances, Coke qualifies the right to use deadly force in defending oneself by requiring the person, whom is attacked, to retreat to the wall. Coke states the rule as follows:

> "If A be assaulted by B, and they fight together, and before any mortal blow be given, A giveth back until he cometh to a hedge, wall, or other strait, beyond which he can not passe, and then, in his own defense and for safeguard of his own life, killeth the other; this is voluntary, and yet no felony; and the jury that finde that it was done *se defendendo*, ought to finde the special matter."[3]

---

[2] Sir Edward Coke, Institutes of the Laws of England (London: E. & R. Brooke, 1794)

[3] Sir Edward Coke, The Third Part of the Institutes of the Laws of England 55-57 (London: 4TH ed., 1669)

However, Coke provides for no duty to retreat upon a fierce attack and further writes that:

> "If A assault B so fiercely and violently and in such manner as if B should give back, he should be in danger of his life, he may, in this case, defende himself; and if, in that defense, he killeth A, it is *se defendendo*." [3]

In addition to having no duty to retreat while under "fierce" attack, Coke writes that one has no duty to retreat when confronted by a attempted thief, robber or murderer and states:

> "Some, without giving back to a wall, etc., or other inevitable cause, as if a thief offer to rob or murder B either abroad or in his house, and thereupon assault him, and B defende himselfe without giving back, and in his defense killeth the thiefe, [*195] this is no felony; for a man shall never give way to a thiefe, etc., neither shall he forfeit anything." [3]

Reading Cokes rule literally, one can understand the requirement to retreat only applied to situations where the attacker did not have a felonious intent (intent to murder, steal, rob, rape, etc.). These circumstances included those beginning with quarrels of words. Therefore, under Coke's rule, one who was attacked with intent to seriously injure him was under no duty to retreat – unless such quarrel be one of merely words.

## Sir Matthew Hale

Sir Matthew Hale (1609-1676), was an influential English barrister, a Member of Parliament, Judge and Jurist.[4]  In 1671 Hale became the Chief Justice of the King's Bench under the reign of King Charles II.  Hale is most known for his treatise The History of the Pleas of the Crown published in 1736.[5]

It is in this Treatise that Hale again describes the notion of a duty to retreat and echoes Coke's exceptions thereto. Hale writes the rule as follows:

> "But in this Homicide *Se Defendendo*, the Party that is assaulted not excused, unless he give back to the Wall. But if the assault be so fierce, and in such a Place, that giving back would endanger his life, then he need not give back."[6]

Hale explains the rule by stating that "if there be malice between A and B and A strike first, B retreats to the wall, and in his own defence kills A this is *Se Defendendo*." Also in comport with Coke's exception to the duty,

---

[4] Gilbert Burnet, The life of Sir Matthew Hale, Knt. 1 (London: C. & J. Rivingston, 1823)

[5] Gilbert Burnet, D.D. & James Loring, Incidents in the Life of Matthew Hale (Boston: 1832)

[6] Sir Matthew Hale, Pleas of the Crown: Second Part, 41-42 (London: 1716)

Hale further writes:

> "In case of a justifiable Homicide, as of a Thief that comes to rob me, or by an Officer resisted in Executing an arrest, the Party need not give back to the Wall."[6]

This rule, complies with Coke's prior writings establishing an exception to the duty to retreat when attacked with a felonious intent. However, Hale categorizes this type of homicide as justifiable rather than excusable.

**Sir William Blackstone**

Sir William Blackstone (1723-1780), a well-known legal scholar, Jurist, and Judge and Member of Parliament is most known for his treatise Commentaries of the Laws of England.[7] In his treatise he expressed the view that any quarrel an Englishman may have with another must be decided peaceably in a court of law. Blackstone provided a more detailed review and explanation of homicide then the prior writings of Coke and Hale. Blackstone separated homicide into three categories, *justifiable*,

---

[7] A Gentlemen of Lincoln's Inn, The Biographical History of Sir William Blackstone, 1-31 (London: 1782)

*excusable*, and *felonious*.[8]

## Justifiable Homicide

The first, justifiable, includes a very narrow class of homicides done in the name of the law. These included 1) Homicide Necessary in the Execution of Justice; 2) Advancement of Public Justice; and 3) Prevention of any Forcible and Atrocious crime.[9]


## Necessary

Homicide necessary in the execution of justice consisted of the execution of those persons convicted and sentenced to death. Such homicides, in order to be justified, must have been executed in the manner prescribed by the decree. If the decree required the felon to be hanged, the execution must be in the form of hanging otherwise it would be considered murder.

---

[8] William C. Sprague, A. B., LL. B., Blackstone Commentaries Abridged (Chicago: 1915)

[9] Sir William Blackstone, The Commentaries of the Laws of England, Book of the Fourth, Chapter XIV, 176-226 (London: 1876)

## For the Advancement of Public Justice

Justifiable homicide in the advancement of public justice included another small class of homicides dealing with maintaining public order. These included:

1.   An officer, in the execution of his duties, killing another who assaults him;

2.   A person who, in attempting to take a man charged with a felony, if resisted by him, kills him; and

3.   An officer who kills a prisoner upon being assaulted by him in an attempt to escape.


## For the Prevention of Atrocious Crimes

The last category of justifiable homicide, Blackstone writes, is homicide done for the prevention of a forcible and atrocious crime. These crimes were limited to the killing of an attempted murderer or robber, or of a person attempting to break in or burn a person's home at night. This category also included the killing of a person attempting to commit rape – but did not include killing of a person committing adultery by consent.

Blackstone's writing of this category of homicide follows those of Coke and Hale. As with Coke and Hale treatises, it does not require a duty to retreat when preventing an atrocious crime (murder, robbery, rape, etc.)

### Excusable Homicide

The second category of homicide, as described by Blackstone, consisted of two types 1) *per misadventure* and 2) *se defendendo*.

### *Per Misadventure*

Homicide per misadventure, also known as per infortunium, is defined as a person, while doing a lawful act, kills another without intent to harm him. These types of homicide included an officer correcting a prisoner, a parent correcting a child, or a master correcting a servant – so long as the moderation of correction did not exceed its bounds.

### *Se Defendendo*

Homicide Se Defendendo, in self-defense, was permitted only in a certain class of circumstances. This category is limited to person's who kill another in self- defense and meet specific requirements. They must not be the aggressor, retreat as far as possible, and bear the burden of proof to show same.

## Felonious Homicide

All other homicides, including the killing of one's self, fell into the last and final category of homicide. These were killings that did not fall into any of the first two categories as they we deemed to be neither justifiable nor excusable.

## Summation of the Duty to Retreat

In sum, the duty to retreat, pertaining to excusable homicide, was stated by Blackstone as follows:

> "[T]he law requires that the person who kills another in his own defence should have retreated as far as he conveniently or safely can to avoid the violence of the assault before he turns upon his assailant"

Blackstone further describes the efforts to retreat by require the party assaulted "flee as far as he conveniently can, either by reason of some **wall**, ditch, or other impediment, or as far as the **fierceness of the assault will permit him**..." (emphasis added).[10]

---

[10] Sir William Blackstone, *The Commentaries of the Laws of England*, Book of the Fourth, Chapter XIV, 208 (London: 1876)

It is perhaps the fierceness description and the category of justifiable homicide in preventing an atrocious crime that led to the latter dispute of the legal scholars as to the requirement of the duty to retreat. It may, however, be the categorization of these defenses that led to latter confusion.

# CHAPTER 2

# AN ATTEMPT TO CLARIFY THE RULE

**Sir Michael Foster**

Sir Michael Foster (1689-1763) Judge of the King's Bench in 1762 authored the influential treatise entitled A Report of Some Proceedings on the Commission for the Trial of the Rebels in the Year 1746, in the Country of Surry; and Other Crown Cases: to which are Added Discourses Upon a Few Branches of the Crown Law – later known more commonly as Foster's Crown Law.[11]

In his Crown Law treatise, Foster categorizes justifiable homicide, as described by Coke, Hale and Blackstone, as justifiable self-defense. Foster points out, in his Crown Law, that homicide founded in necessity falls into two categories se et sua defendendo (in defense of one's self or property),

---

[11] Michael Dodson & John Disney, The Life of Sir Michael Foster, Knt: Sometime One of the Judges of the Court of King's Bench (London: 1811)

for which Foster asserts is perfectly innocent, or that which is barely excusable, committed by one protecting himself when not attacked with felonious intent.[12]

In comport with the views of Coke, Hale and Blackstone, Foster describes justifiable self-defense as follows:

> "In the case of justifiable self-defense, the injured party may repel force with force in defense of his person, habitation or property, against one who manifestly intendeth and endeavoreth, with violence or surprise, to commit a known felony upon either. In these cases he is not obliged to retreat, but may pursue his adversary till he findeth himself out of danger, and if, in a conflict between them, he happeneth to kill, such killing is justifiable." *Id* at 273

Foster, as did the prior scholars on the subject, recognized that in some cases the accused could not avail himself to the protections of justifiable self-defense. In describing excusable homicide, Foster writes:

> "...there are cases in which the defendant can not avail himself of the plea of self-defense without showing that he retreated as far as he could with safety, and then, merely for the preservation of his own life, killed the assailant. This I call self-defense, culpable, but, through the benignity of the law, excusable." *Id* at 273

Foster seems to blame the confusion of the issue on prior scholars not

---

[12] Sir Michael Foster, A Report of Some Proceedings on the Commission for the Trial of the Rebels in the Year 1746, 273 (3rd ed. 1792)

specifically identifying the type of cases involved in excusable homicide. Foster urges that excusable homicide is only found where two parties fight on equal terms and one, after repudiating the battle, retreats to the wall before striking the mortal wound upon his adversary.

Foster also bases his theory of self-defense as being founded in the law of nature. The right to self-defense, Foster says, cannot be superseded by any law of society. He also points that such a right was, prior to the civil societies being formed, an individual right. *Id* at 274

## Edward Hyde East

Edward Hyde East (1764-1847) was a British Member of Parliament, legal scholar, and Judge in India. He served as Chief Justice of Calcutta from 1813 to 1822. In 1803, after almost fifteen years of research and writing, East wrote his treatise of the *Pleas of the Crown*.[13]

East, in his *Pleas of the Crown*, also speaks of justifiable and excusable homicide and defines them similarly to Foster.[14] In defining justifiable homicide, East writes:

> "A man may repel force by force, in defense of his person, habitation, or property, against one who manifestly intends and endeavors, by violence or surprise, to commit a known

---

[13] 13 Dictionary of National Biography, 1885–1900. London: Smith, Elder & Co. (2010)

[14] 14 Edward Hyde East, Esq., Pleas of the Crown 198-223, 271-294 (London: 1803)

felony, such as murder, rape, robbery, arson, burglary, and the like, upon either. In these cases he is not obliged to retreat, but may pursue his adversary until he has secured himself from all danger; and if he kill him in so doing it is called justifiable self-defense"
*Id* at 271

East also defines excusable homicide, as did Foster, when "death ensues from a combat between parties on a sudden quarrel." This comports with the distinction Foster made in explaining his view of excusable homicide vs. justifiable homicide not carefully expounded upon by Coke, Hale and Blackstone.

# CHAPTER 3

# AMERICA ADOPTS FOSTER-EAST DOCTRINE

In Beard v. US, 158 U.S. 550 (1985), the Defendant had a dispute with three brothers over the ownership of a cow. During the argument, one of the brothers walked towards the defendant in an aggressive manner with his left hand in his pocket. The defendant warned him to stop and he continued towards him. The defendant struck him in the head killing him. The Supreme Court set the rule of law as follows:

> A man may repel force by force, in defence of his person, habitation or property, against one who manifestly intends or endeavors, by violence or surprise, to commit a known felony, such as murder, rape, robbery, arson, burglary, and the like, upon either. In these cases he is not obliged to retreat, but may pursue his adversary until he has secured himself from all danger; and if he kill him in so doing it is called justifiable self-defence; as, on the other hand, the killing by such felon of any person so lawfully defending himself will be murder. But a bare fear of any of these offences, however well grounded, as that another lies in wait to take away the party's life, unaccompanied with any overt act indicative of such an intention, will not warrant

in killing that other by way of prevention. There must be an actual danger at the time. In the case of justifiable self-defence, the injured party may repel force with force in defence of his person, habitation, or property, against one who manifestly intendeth and endeavoreth, with violence or surprise, to commit a known felony upon either. In these cases he is not obliged to retreat, but may pursue his adversary till he findeth himself out of danger, and if, in a conflict between them, he happeneth to kill, such killing is justifiable. *Id* at 599.

In *Beard*, the Supreme Court considered the works of the above mentioned legal scholars and took the view of Foster and East, thus developing the Foster-East Doctrine of no duty to retreat. In reality, the difference in the views cannot be examined without splitting hairs. The *Beard* case in its entirety follows.

## Beard v. United States, 158 U.S. 550 (1895)

Mr. Justice HARLAN delivered the opinion of the court.

The plaintiff in error, a white man, and not an Indian, was indicted in the circuit court of the United States for the *551 Western district of Arkansas for the crime of having killed and murdered, in the Indian country, and within that district, one Will Jones, also a white person, and not an Indian.

He was found guilty of manslaughter, and, a motion for a new trial having been overruled, it was adjudged that he be imprisoned in Kings County Penitentiary, at Brooklyn, N. Y., for the term of eight years, and pay to the United States a fine of $500.

The record contains a bill of exceptions embodying all the evidence, as well as the charge of the court to the jury, and the requests of the accused for instructions. To certain parts of the charge, and to the action of the court in refusing instructions asked by the defendant, exceptions were duly taken.

The principal question in the case arises out of those parts of the charge in which the court instructed the jury as to the principles of the law of self-defense.

There was evidence before the jury tending to establish the following facts:

An angry dispute arose between Beard and three brothers by the name of Jones-Will Jones, John Jones, and Edward Jones-in reference to a cow, which a few years before that time, and just after the death of his mother, was set apart to Edward. The children, being without any means for their support, were distributed among their relatives, Edward being assigned to Beard, whose wife was a sister of Mrs. Jones. Beard took him into his family upon the condition that he should have the right to control him and the cow as if the lad were one of his own children and the cow his own property. At the time Edward went to live with Beard he was only eight or nine years of age, poorly clad, and not in good physical condition.

After remaining some years with his aunt and uncle, Edward Jones left the Beard house, and determined, with the aid of his older brothers, to take the cow with him, each of them knowing that the accused objected to that being done.

The Jones brothers, one of them taking a shotgun with him, went upon the premises of the accused for the purpose of taking the cow away, whether Beard consented or not. *552 But they were prevented by the accused from accomplishing that object, and he warned them not to come to his place again for such a purpose, informing them that, if Edward Jones was entitled to the possession of the cow, he could have it, provided his claim was successfully asserted through legal proceedings instituted by or in his behalf.

Will Jones, the oldest of the brothers, and about 20 or 21 years of age, publicly avowed his intention to get the cow away from the Beard farm or kill Beard, and of that threat the latter was informed on the day preceding that on which the fatal difficulty in question occurred.

In the afternoon of the day on which the Jones brothers were warned by Beard not again to come upon his premises for the cow unless attended by an officer of the law, and in defiance of that warning, they again went to his farm, in his absence,-one of them, the deceased, being armed with a concealed deadly weapon,-and attempted to take the cow away, but were prevented from doing so by Mrs. Beard, who drove it back into the lot from which it was being taken.

While the Jones brothers were on the defendant's premises in the afternoon, for the purpose of taking the cow away, Beard returned to his home from a town near by,-having with him a shotgun that he was in the habit of carrying when absent from home,-and went at once from his dwelling into the lot called the 'orchard lot,' a distance of about 50 or 60 yards from his house, and near to that part of an adjoining field or lot where the cow was, and in which the Jones brothers and Mrs. Beard were at the time of the difficulty.

Beard ordered the Jones brothers to leave his premises. They refused to leave. Thereupon Will Jones, who was on the opposite side of the orchard fence, 10 or 15 yards only from Beard, moved towards the latter with an angry manner and in a brisk walk, having his left hand (he being, as Beard knew, left-handed) in the left pocket of his trousers. When he got within five or six steps of Beard, the latter warned him to stop, but he did not do so. As he approached nearer the accused asked him what he intended to do, and he replied, 'Damn you. I will show you,' at the same time making a *553 movement with his left hand as if to draw a pistol **963 from his pocket, whereupon the accused struck him over the head with his gun, and knocked him down.

'Believing,' the defendant testified, 'from his demonstrations just mentioned that he intended to shoot me, I struck him over the head with my gun, to prevent him killing me. As soon as I struck him, his brother John, who was a few steps behind him, started towards me with his hand in his pocket. Believing that he intended to take part in the difficulty, and was also armed, I struck him, and he stopped. I then at once jumped over the fence, caught Will Jones by the lapel of the coat, turned him rather to one side, and pulled his left hand out of his pocket. He had a pistol, which I found in his pocket, grasped in his left hand, and I pulled his pistol and his left hand out together. My purpose in doing this was to disarm him, to prevent him from shooting me, as I did not know how badly he was hurt. My gun was loaded, having ten cartridges in the magazine. I could have shot him, but did not want to kill him, believing that I could knock him down with the gun, and disarm him, and protect myself without shooting him. After getting his pistol, John Jones said something to me about killing him, to which I replied that I had not killed him, and did not try to do so, for if I had I could have shot him. He said my gun was not loaded. Thereupon I shot the gun in the air to show him that it was loaded.'

Dr. Howard Hunt, a witness, on behalf of the government, testified that he called to see Will Jones soon after he was hurt, and found him in a serious condition; that he died from the effects of a wound given by the defendant; that the wound was across the head, rather on the right side, the skull being crushed by the blow. He saw the defendant soon after dressing the wound, and told him that the deceased's condition was serious; and that he, the witness, was sorry the occurrence had happened. The witness suggested to the accused that perhaps he had better get out of the way. The latter replied that he was sorry that it had happened, but that he acted in self-defense, and would not go away. Beard seemed *554 a little offended at the suggestion that he should run off, and observed to the witness that the latter could not scare him, for he was perfectly justified in what he did. This witness further testified that he had known the defendant four or five years, was well acquainted in the neighborhood in which he lived, and knew his general reputation, which was that of a peaceable, law-abiding man.

The account we have given of the difficulty is not in harmony, is every particular, with the testimony of some of the witnesses, but it is sustained by what the accused and others testified to at the trial; so that, if the jury had found the facts to be as we have detailed them, it could not have been said that their finding was contrary to the evidence. At any rate, it was the duty of the court to tell the jury by what principles of law they should be guided, in the event they found the facts to be as stated by the accused.

Assuming, then, that the facts were as we have represented them to be, we are to inquire whether the court erred in its charge to the jury. In the view we take of the case, it will be necessary to refer to those parts only of the charge relating to the law of self-defense.

The court stated at considerable length the general rules that determine whether the killing of a human being is murder or manslaughter, and, among other things, said to the jury: 'If these boys, or young men, or whatever you may consider them, went down there and they were there unlawfully,-if they had no right to go there,-you naturally inquire whether the defendant was placed in such a situation as that he could kill for that reason. Of course, he could not. He could not kill them because they were upon his place. * * * And if these young men were there in the act of attempting the larceny of this cow and calf, and the defendant killed because of that, because his mind was inflamed for the reason that they were seeking to do an act of that kind, that is manslaughter. That is all it is. There is nothing else in it. That is considered so far provocative as that it reduces the grade of the crime to manslaughter, and no further. If they had no intent to commit a larceny; if it was a bare, naked trespass; if they were there *555 under a claim of right to get this cow, though they may not have had any right to it, but in good faith they were exercising their claim of that kind, and Will Jones was killed by the defendant for that reason,-that would be murder, because you cannot kill a man for bare trespass,-you cannot take his life for a bare trespass,-and say the act is mitigated.'

After restating the proposition that a man cannot take life because of mere fear on his part, or in order that he may prevent the commission of a bare trespass, the court proceeded: 'Now, a word further upon the proposition that I have already adverted to as to what was his duty at the time. If that danger was real, coming from the hands of Will Jones, or it was apparent as coming from his hands, and as affecting this defendant by some overt act at the time, was the defendant called upon to avoid that danger by getting out of the way of it if he could? The court says he was. The court tells you that he was. There is but one place where he need not retreat any further, where he need not go away from the danger, and that is in his dwelling house. He may be upon his own premises, and if a man, while so situated, and upon his own premises, can do that which would reasonably put aside the danger short of taking life, if he can do that, I say, he is called upon to do so by retreating, **964 by getting out of the way if he can, by avoiding a conflict that may be about to come upon him; and the law says that he must do so; and the fact that he is standing upon his own premises away from his own dwelling house does not take away from him the exercise of the duty of avoiding the danger if he can with a due regard to his own safety by getting away from there, or by resorting to some other means of less violence than those resorted to. Now, the rule as applicable to a man of that kind upon his own premises-upon his own property, but outside of his dwelling house-is as I have just stated.' Again: 'You are to bear in mind that the first proposition of the law of self-defense was that the defendant in this case was in the lawful pursuit of his business; that is to say, he was doing what he had a right to do at the time. If he was not, he deprives himself of the right of self-defense, and, no matter what his adversary may do, if he, *556 by his own conduct, creates certain conditions by his own wrongful conduct, he cannot take advantage of such conditions, created by his own wrongful act or acts. * * * Again, going to the place where the person slain is, with a deadly weapon, for the purpose of provoking a difficulty or with the intent of having an affray. Now, if a man does that, he is in the wrong, and he is cut off from the right of self-defense, no matter what his adversary may do, because the law says in the very language of these propositions relating to the law of self-defense that he must avoid taking life if he can with due regard to his own safety. Whenever he can do that he must do it. Therefore, if he has an adversary, and he knows that there is a bitter feeling-that there is a state of feeling that may precipitate a deadly conflict-between himself and his adversary, while he has a right to pursue his usual daily avocations that are right and proper, going about his business, to go and do what is necessary to be done in that way, yet, if he knows that condition I have named to exist, and he goes to the place where the slain person is, with a deadly weapon, for the purpose of provoking a difficulty, or with the intent of having an affray,-if it comes up, he is there to have it,-and he acts for that purpose, the law says there is no self-defense for him. * * * If he went to the place where that young man was, armed with a deadly weapon, even if it was upon his own premises, with the purpose of provoking a difficulty with him, in which he might use that deadly weapon, or of having a deadly affray with him, it does not make any difference what was done by the young man; there is no self-defense for the defendant. The law of self-defense does not apply to a case of that kind, because he cannot be the creator of a wrong,-of a wrong state of case,-and then act upon it. Now, if either one of these conditions exists, I say, the law of self-defense does not apply in this case.'

Later in the charge, the court recurred to the inquiry as to what the law demanded of Beard before striking the deceased with his gun, and said: 'If at the time of this killing it be true that the deceased was doing an act of apparent or real deadly violence, and that state of case existed, and yet that *557 the defendant at the time could have avoided the necessity of taking his life by the exercise of any other reasonable means, and he did not do that, because he did not exercise other reasonable means that would have with equal certainty saved his life, but resorted to this dernier remedy, under those facts and circumstances the law says he is guilty of manslaughter. Now, let us see what that requires. It requires: First, that the proof must show that Will Jones was doing an act of violence or about to do it, or apparently doing it or about to do it, but that it was an act that the defendant could have escaped from by doing something else other than taking the life of Jones, by getting out of the way of that danger, as he was called upon to do, as I have already told you, for he could not stand there as he could stand in his own dwelling house, and he must have reasonably sought to avoid that danger before he took the life of Jones; and if he did not do that, if you find that to be Jones' position from this testimony, and he could have done so, but did not do it, the defendant would be guilty of manslaughter when he took the life of Jones, because in that kind of a case the law says that the conduct of Jones would be so provocative as to reduce the grade of crime. Yet, at the same time, it was a state of case that the defendant could have avoided without taking his life, and because he did not do it he is guilty of the crime of manslaughter.' Further: 'If it be true that Will Jones, at the time he was killed, was exercising deadly violence, or about to do so, or apparently exercising it, or apparently about to do so, and the defendant could have paralyzed the effect of that violence without taking the life of Jones, but he did not do it, but resorted to this deadly violence, when he could have protected his own life without resorting to that dernier remedy,-if that be the state of the case,-the law says he is guilty of manslaughter, because he is doing that which he had no right to do. This great law of self-defense commands him at all times to do that which he can do under the circumstances, to wit, exercise reasonable care to avoid the danger by getting out of the way of it, or by exercising less violence than that which will produce death, and yet will be equally efiective to secure his own life. If either of *558 these propositions exist,-and they must exist to the extent I have defined to you, and the defendant took the life of Jones under these circumstances, the defendant would be guilty of manslaughter.'

We are of opinion that the charge of the court to the jury was objectionable, in point of law, on several grounds.

There was no evidence tending to show that Beard went from his dwelling house to the orchard fence for the purpose of provoking **965 a difficulty, or with the intent of having an affray with the Jones brothers, or with either of them. On the contrary, from the outset of the dispute he evinced a purpose to avoid a difficulty or an affray. He expressed his willingness to abide by the law in respect to his right to retain the cow in his possession. He warned the Jones brothers, as he had a legal right to do, against coming upon his premises for the purpose of taking the cow away. They disregarded this warning, and determined to take the law into their own hands, whatever might be the consequences of such a course. Nevertheless, when Beard came to where they were, near the orchard fence, he did nothing to provoke a difficulty, and prior to the moment when he struck Will Jones with his gun he made no demonstration that indicated any desire whatever on his part to engage in an affray, or to have an angry controversy. He only commanded them, as he had the legal right to do, to leave his premises. He neither used, nor threatened to use, force against them.

The court several times, in its charge, raised or suggested the inquiry whether Beard was in the lawful pursuit of his business-that is, doing what he had a right to do-when, after returning home in the afternoon, he went from his dwelling house to a part of his premises near the orchard fence, just outside of which his wife and the Jones brothers were engaged in a dispute; the former endeavoring to prevent the cow from being taken away, the latter trying to drive it off the premises. Was he not doing what he had the legal right to do, when, keeping within his own premises, and near his dwelling, he joined his wife, who was in dispute with others, one of whom, as he had been informed, had already threatened to take *559 the cow away or kill him? We have no hesitation in answering this question in the affirmative.

The court also said: 'The use of provoking language, or, it seems, resorting to any other device, in order to get another to commence an assault so as to have a pretext for taking his life, agreeing with another to fight him with a deadly weapon, either one of these cases, if they exist as the facts in this case, puts the case in such an attitude that there is no self-defense in it.' We are at a loss to understand why any such hypothetical cases were put before the jury. The jury must have supposed that, in the opinion of the court, there was evidence showing that Beard sought an opportunity to do physical harm to the Jones boys, or to some one of them. There was not the slightest foundation in the evidence for the intimation that Beard had used provoking language, or resorted to any device, in order to have a pretext to take the life of either of the brothers. Much less was there any reason to believe that there was an agreement to fight with deadly weapons.

But the court below committed an error of a more serious character when it told the jury, as in effect it did by different forms of expression, that if the accused could have saved his own life and avoided the taking of the life of Will Jones by retreating from and getting out of the way of the latter as he advanced upon him, the law made it his duty to do so; and if he did not, when it was in his power to do so without putting his own life or body in imminent peril, he was guilty of manslaughter. The court seemed to think, if the deceased had advanced upon the accused while the latter was in his dwelling house, and under such circumstances as indicated the intention of the former to take life or inflict great bodily injury, and if, without retreating, the accused had taken the life of his assailant, having at the time reasonable grounds to believe, and in good faith believing, that his own life would be taken, or great bodily harm done him, unless he killed the accused, the case would have been one of justifiable homicide. To that proposition we give our entire assent. But we cannot agree that the accused was under any greater obligation when on his own premises, near his dwelling house, to retreat or run away *560 from his assailant, than he would have been if attacked within his dwelling house. The accused being where he had a right to be, on his own premises, constituting a part of his residence and home, at the time the deceased approached him in a threatening manner, and not having by language or by conduct provoked the deceased to assault him, the question for the jury was whether, without fleeing from his adversary, he had, at the moment he struck the deceased, reasonable grounds to believe, and in good faith believed, that he could not save his life or protect himself from great bodily harm except by doing what he did, namely, strike the deceased with his gun, and thus prevent his further advance upon him. Even if the jury had been prepared to answer this question in the affirmative,-and if it had been so answered the defendant should have been acquitted,-they were instructed that the accused could not properly be acquitted on the ground of self-defense if they believed that by retreating from his adversary, by 'getting out of the way,' he could have avoided taking life. We cannot give our assent to this doctrine.

The application of the doctrine of 'retreating to the wall' was carefully examined by the supreme court of Ohio in Erwin v. State, 29 Ohio St. 186, 193, 199. That was an indictment for murder; the defendant being found guilty. The trial court charged the jury that if the defendant was in the lawful pursuit of his business at the time the fatal shot was fired, and was attacked by the deceased under circumstances denoting an intention to take life or do great bodily harm, he could lawfully kill his assailant, provided he used all means 'in his power' otherwise  \*\*966 to save his own life or prevent the intended harm, 'such as retreating as far as he can, or disabling his adversary without killing him, if it be in his power'; that if the attack was so sudden, fierce, and violent that a retreat would not diminish, but increase, the defendant's danger, he might kill his adversary without retreating; and, further that if from the character of the attack there was reasonable ground for the defendant to believe, and he did honestly believe, that his life was about to be taken, or he was to suffer great bodily harm, and that he believed honestly that he would be in equal danger \*561 by retreating, then, if he took the life of the assailant, he was excused. Of this charge the accused complained.

Upon a full review of the authorities, and looking to the principles of the common law as expounded by writers and courts of high authority, the supreme court of Ohio held that the charge was erroneous, saying: 'It is true that all authorities agree that the taking of life in defense of one's person cannot be either justified or excused except on the ground of necessity, and that such necessity must be imminent at the time; and they also agree that no man can avail himself of such necessity if he brings it upon himself. The question, then, is simply this: Does the law hold a man who is violently and feloniously assaulted responsible for having brought such necessity upon himself on the sole ground that he failed to fly from his assailant when he might safely have done so? The law, out of tenderness for human life and the frailties of human nature, will not permit the taking of it to repel a mere trespass, or even to save life where the assault is provoked; but a true man, who is without fault, is not obliged to fly from an assailant, who by violence or surprise maliciously seeks to take his life, or to do him enormous bodily harm. Now, under the charge below, notwithstanding the defendant may have been without fault, and, so assaulted, with the necessity of taking life to save his own upon him, still the jury could not have acquitted if they found he failed to do all in his power otherwise to save his own life, or prevent the intended harm, as retreating as far as he could, etc. In this case, we think, the law was not

24

correctly stated.'

In Runyan v. State, 57 Ind. 80, 83, which was an indictment for murder, and where the instructions of the trial court involved the present question, the court said: 'A very brief examination of the American authorities makes it evident that the ancient doctrine as to the duty of a person assailed to retreat as far as he can before he is justified in repelling force by force has been greatly modified in this country, and has with us a much narrower application than formerly. Indeed, the tendency of the American mind seems to be very strongly against the enforcement of any rule which *562 requires a person to flee when assailed, to avoid chastisement, or even to save human life; and that tendency is well illustrated by the recent decisions of our courts bearing on the general subject of the right of self-defense. The weight of modern authority, in our judgment, establishes the doctrine that when a person, being without fault, and in a place where he has a right to be, is violently assaulted, he may, without retreating, repel force by force, and if, in the reasonable exercise of his right of self-defense, his assailant is killed, he is justifiable. * * * It seems to us that the real question in the case, when it was given to the jury, was whether the defendant, under all the circumstances, was justified in the use of a deadly weapon in repelling the assault of the deceased. We mean by this, did the defendant have reason to believe, and did he in fact believe, that what he did was necessary for the safety of his own life, or to protect him from great bodily harm? On that question the law is simple and easy of solution, as has been already seen from the authorities cited above.'

In East's Pleas of the Crown, the author, considering what sort of an attack it was lawful and justifiable to resist, even by the death of the assailant, says: 'A man may repel force by force in defense of his person, habitation, or property against one who manifestly intends and endeavors, by violence or surprise, to commit a known felony, such as murder, rape, robbery, arson, burglary, and the like, upon either. In these cases he is not obliged to retreat, but may pursue his adversary until he has secured himself from all danger; and if he kill him in so doing it is called justifiable self-defense; as, on the other hand, the killing by such felon of any person so lawfully defending himself will be murder. But a bare fear of any of these offenses, however well grounded,-as that another lies in wait to take away the party's life,-unaccompanied with any overt act indicative of such an intention, will not warrant in killing that other by way of prevention. There must be an actual danger at the time.' Page 271. So in Foster's Crown Cases: 'In the case of justifiable self-defense, the injured party may repel force with force in defense of his person *563 habitation, or property against one who manifestly intendeth and endeavoreth, with violence or surprise, to commit a known felony upon either. In these cases he is not obliged to retreat, but may pursue his adversary till he findeth himself out of danger, and if, in a conflict between them, he happeneth to kill, such killing is justifiable.' Chapter 3, p. 273.

In Bishop's Criminal Law, the author, after observing that cases of mere assault and of mutual quarrel, where the attacking party has not the purpose of murder in his heart, are those to which is applied the doctrine of the books that one cannot justify the **967 killing of another, though apparently in self-defense, unless he retreat to the wall or other interposing obstacle before resorting to this extreme right, says that: 'Where an attack is made with murderous intent, there being sufficient overt act, the person attacked is under no duty to fly. He may stand his ground, and, if need be, kill his adversary. And it is the same where the attack is with a deadly weapon, for in this case a person attacked may well assume that the other intends murder, whether he does in fact or not.' Volume 1, § 850. The rule is thus expressed by Wharton: 'A man may repel force by force in defense of his person, habitation, or property against any one or many who manifestly intend and endeavor to commit a known felony by violence or surprise or either. In such case he is not compelled to retreat, but may pursue his adversary until he finds himself out of danger; and if, in the conflict between them he happen to kill him, such killing is justifiable.' 2 Whart. Cr. Law, § 1019.

See, also, Gallagher v. State, 3 Minn. 270, 273 (Gil. 185); Pond v. People, 8 Mich. 150, 177; State v. Dixon, 75 N. C. 275, 279; State v. Sherman, 16 R. I. 631, 18 Atl. 1040; Fields v. State (Ind. Sup.) 32 N. E. 780; Eversole v. Com. (Ky.) 26 S. W. 816; Haynes v. State, 17 Ga. 465, 483; Long v. State, 52 Miss. 23, 35; State v. Tweedy, 5 Iowa, 433; Baker v. Com. (Ky.) 19 S. W. 975; Tingle v. Com. (Ky.) 11 S. W. 812; 3 Rice, Ev. § 360.

In our opinion, the court below erred in holding that the accused, while on his premises, outside of his dwelling house, was under a legal duty to get out of the way, if he could, of *564 his assailant, who, according to one view of the evidence, had threatened to kill the defendant, in execution of that purpose had armed himself with a deadly weapon, with that weapon concealed upon his person went to the defendant's premises, despite the warning of the latter to keep away, and by word and act indicated his purpose to attack the accused. The defendant was where he had the right to be, when the deceased advanced upon him in a threatening manner, and with a deadly weapon; and if the accused did not provoke the assault, and had at the time reasonable grounds to believe, and in good faith believed, that the deceased intended to take his life, or do him great bodily harm, he was not obliged to retreat, nor to consider whether he could safely retreat, but was entitled to stand his ground, and meet any attack made upon him with a deadly weapon, in such way and with such force as, under all the circumstances, he, at the moment, honestly believed, and had reasonable grounds to believe, were necessary to save his own life, or to protect himself from great bodily injury.

As the proceedings below were not conducted in accordance with these principles, the judgment must be reversed, and the cause remanded, with directions to grant a new trial.

Other objections to the charge of the court are raised by the assignments of error, but, as the questions which they present may not arise upon another trial, they will not be now examined. Judgment reversed.

Jason C. King

# CHAPTER 4

## FLORIDA AND THE
## COMMON LAW DUTY TO RETREAT

Florida case law long recognized the common law duty to retreat. In 1905, the Florida Supreme Court approved a lower courts use of a jury instruction with the following phrase "used all other reasonable means in his power, consistent with his own safety, to avert the danger" which encompassed the common law duty to retreat.[15]

In the case of *Stafford v. State*, 50 Fla. 134 (1905), the Court discussed the burden of the accused, when arguing self-defense, and stated that he must show he used all reasonable means to avoid the danger. The ruling held that: "to justify his acts on the ground of self-defense, must have used all reasonable means within his power and consistent with his own safety to avoid danger and to avert the necessity of taking the life of the deceased…"

---

[15] *Snelling v. State*, 49 Fla. 34 (1905)

However, as will be discussed in Chapter 6, the Florida Legislature enacted statutes that removed the common law duty to retreat in 2005. The statute unequivocally removed the common law duty to retreat. Following the amendment, several cases have discussed its removal.

## Snelling v. State, 49 Fla. 34 (1905)

Error to Circuit Court, Jackson County; Lucius J. Reeves, Judge.

Loren Snelling was convicted of manslaughter, and appeals. Affirmed.

### Syllabus by the Court

1. Immaterial and irrelevant questions on cross-examination are properly excluded upon objection duly made, and answers to questions on cross-examination, when immaterial, are properly stricken on motion.

2. An official court reporter for the circuit court, under the statutes of this state, may testify in rebuttal as a evidence given at a preliminary hearing before a committing magistrate, when the testimony is given independently of any record, or from memory as refreshed by a transcript of notes taken by the witness at the preliminary hearing.

3. It is not error to refuse instructions containing propositions already substantially given in charges, though couched in different language.

4. Where the court has given a proper charge on the subject of reasonable doubt, it is not error to refuse a requested charge that 'to justify a jury in finding a verdict of unlawful homicide, in any of its degrees, against the defendant, each individual juror must be convinced from the evidence, for himself, that the defendant is so guilty.'

5. In a prosecution for murder, it is not error to add to a charge on the subject of self-defense requested by the defendant the following: 'Provided he had used all reasonable means within his power, consistent with his own safety, to avert the danger and avoid the necessity of taking P.'s life.'

6. In a prosecution for murder of one Pridgeon, where the question of self-defense was raised by the testimony, the court refused to give the following charge as requested by the defendant: 'If you should believe from the evidence that the defendant was free from fault in bringing on the difficulty, and was not the aggressor therein, and that he was assaulted by the deceased, or by the deceased and another, who were armed with deadly weapons, and that such assault was made under such circumstances that it reasonably appeared to the defendant, as an ordinarily cautious and prudent man, that he was in danger of death or great bodily harm at the hands of the deceased, or of the deceased and another, as aforesaid, then you are instructed that, under such circumstances, it would not be incumbent upon the defendant to flee in order to avoid the difficulty or avert the necessity of taking the life of his assailant; but, on the other hand, under such circumstances, he might lawfully stand his ground, and, if assaulted by the deceased, or the deceased and another, under the circumstances aforesaid, then, in such event, he would be justified in his acts, and you would find him not guilty.' But the court did give the charge with the following added thereto: 'Provided he had used all other reasonable means in his power, consistent with his own safety, to avert the danger, and to avoid the necessity of taking P.'s life.' The charge as modified and given was not inconsistent or misleading, and was not error.

## Opinion

WHITFIELD, C. J.

The plaintiff in error was indicted for the murder of Wylie Pridgeon, and convicted of manslaughter, in the circuit court for Jackson county, and brings this writ of error from the judgment.

*36 The first witness for the state at the trial testified that he, the deceased, Manual Ham, and a woman called 'Janie' were in the 'shanty that Loren Snelling was staying in at the time,' when Loren Snelling entered the shanty, asked why they were there, and ordered them out; that all came out, and soon thereafter the homicide occurred. On cross-examination this witness was asked the question (referring to the deceased), 'Do you know whether or not he had been warned by Mr. Campbell not to come there?' The bill of exceptions then recites: 'To which question the state attorney objected on the ground that the same was immaterial and irrelevant. The defendant offered to prove that the deceased was a trespasser in the house, and that he could follow it up and show that he was a trespasser, and that he was also an intruder on the place, where he had been warned off, and that the deceased was unlawfully there. The court sustained the objection, to which ruling of the court the defendant excepted.' Error is assigned on this ruling. On cross-examination this witness testified: 'When Snelling came, me and Wylie [the deceased] were looking at Janie and Manuel Ham gambling with cards.' Then followed the question: 'Were they gambling?' Answer: 'Yes, sir.' The state attorney moved to strike this answer as being immaterial. The defendant asked that it be not stricken out, on the ground that it showed the motive of the defendant for ordering them from the house; that he had a right to order them from his house if they were gambling. The court sustained the motion, and an exception was noted. This is assigned as error.

The court permitted the defendant to prove that deceased was a trespasser while in the house occupied by the defendant.

*37 There was no attempt to show that the defendant had forbidden the deceased to go on Campbell's premises, or that defendant represented Campbell in respect to any warning he may have given deceased. Consequently the question first above quoted was immaterial and irrelevant, and was properly excluded.

The answer to the second question above quoted was properly excluded as immaterial, since it did not appear that the deceased was gambling in the house.

**918 A witness for the defendant was by the defense asked the question: 'Do you know whether or not Wylie Pridgeon [the deceased] had been forbidden to go on these premises?' An objection by the state to this question was sustained, and an exception noted. The question was not limited to the inquiry whether the defendant had lawfully forbidden the deceased to go on the premises, and it was properly excluded. The same witness was asked by the defense, 'Do you know what his [deceased's] business was?' and 'What was his business?' The difficulty between the defendant and the deceased did not arise from discussing any business matter. These questions were clearly immaterial, as the business of the deceased had no material bearing on defendant's guilt or innocence of the crime for which he was being tried, and they were properly excluded.

The state, in rebuttal, called a witness who testified that she was an official court reporter. She was asked by the state whether she reported the case before the committing magistrate. This question was objected to on the ground that the law providing for a court reporter does not provide for reporting cases in any court except circuit courts. The witness testified that she took the testimony in the case referred to in her capacity as a stenographer *38 or shorthand reporter, generally, under the direction of the judge. The objections to her testimony were that she could not, under the law, officially report a case in a committing magistrate's court so as to make it evidence of itself, and that she could not refresh her memory by the use of a transcript of her notes taken at the trial. There was no attempt to use the notes as evidence. The witness testified that she was able to state what the testimony was at the preliminary hearing referred to by refreshing her memory from the transcript which she made from the shorthand notes taken at the time, and that it was an exact, literal transcript made by her from the notes. The witness was permitted to read from the transcript, but the court afterwards ruled that this 'record' be stricken out, and permitted the testimony of the witness as to what the defendant testified to at the preliminary examination to remain in evidence for consideration by the jury. The testimony of the witness from memory, given independently of any record, of as refreshed by the transcript of her notes, was proper testimony in rebuttal, since it depended upon her knowledge and recollection, and not upon the notes or transcript. The memory of the witness could be refreshed by a literal transcript made by her of the notes taken by her at the preliminary hearing. Davis v. State (Fla.) 36 South. 170.

Exceptions were taken to charges requested by the defendant and refused by the court upon the questions of presumption of innocence, reasonable doubt, and consideration of the evidence given by the defense and by the state. These subjects were fully covered by the general charge of the court, and it was not error to refuse the charges requested.

*39 Error is assigned on the refusal of the court to give the following charge requested by the defendant: 'To justify a jury in finding a verdict of unlawful homicide, in any of its degrees, against the defendant, each individual must be convinced from the evidence, for himself, that the defendant is so guilty.' The court gave a proper charge on the subject of reasonable doubt, and the refusal to give the requested charge quoted above was not error. Baldwin v. State (Fla.) 35 South. 220; Cook v. State (Fla.) 35 South. 665; Smith v. State (Fla.) 37 South. 573.

Exception was taken to the refusal of the court to give a charge requested by the defendant on the subject of self-defense, and also to the giving of the charge with this addition: 'Provided he had used all reasonable means within his power, consistent with his own safety, to avert the danger and avoid the necessity of taking Pridgeon's life.'

The defendant cannot complain of a charge given at his request unless the modification of it by the court before giving it made it erroneous. The language of the modification made by the court in the proviso above quoted has been approved by this court in the case of Peaden v. State (Fla.) 35 South. 204, and we now hold that there was no error in refusing to give the charge as requested, nor in giving the charge as modified.

The court refused to give a charge requested by the defendant, but did give it with the following added thereto: 'Provided he had used all other reasonable means in his power, consistent with his own safety, to avert the danger and to avoid the necessity of taking Pridgeon's life.' The charge, as requested to be given, is: 'If you should believe from the evidence that the defendant was free from fault *40 in bringing on the difficulty, and was not the aggressor therein, and that he was assaulted by the deceased, or by the deceased and another, who were armed with deadly weapons, and that such assault was made under such circumstances that it reasonably appeared to the defendant, as an ordinarily cautious and prudent man, that he was in danger of death or great bodily harm at the hands of the deceased, or of the deceased and another, as aforesaid, then you are instructed that, under such circumstances, it would not be incumbent upon the defendant to flee in order to avoid the difficulty or avert the necessity of taking the life of his assailant; but, on the other hand, under such circumstances, he might lawfully stand his ground, and, if assaulted by the deceased, or the deceased and another, under the circumstances aforesaid, then, in such event, he would be justified in his acts, and you would find him not guilty.' It is contended that the charge as given, while it instructs the jury that the defendant, when so assaulted, is not compelled to retreat before he can invoke **919 in justification for taking the life of his assailant the right of self-defense, yet, by means of the proviso added thereto, it is made the duty of the defendant, before he can rely upon self-defense for vindication of his act, to use all reasonable means in his power, whether by retreat, withdrawing from the difficulty, or otherwise, and thus that the proviso neutralizes the effect of the charge as to the duty to retreat. The bill of exceptions shows the modification contained the words 'all other reasonable means in his power.' This being so, the modification of the charge was not at all inconsistent with the other portions of the charge, and it was not misleading. There was therefore no error in refusing to give the charge as requested, nor in giving it with the modification *41 stated above. In disposing of this assignment of error, the court does not express an opinion whether, under the circumstances stated in the charge, the defendant would be required to retreat if it could safely be done. If so required, then the charge was too favorable to the accused, of which he could not complain. If not so required, the charge as modified fully preserves the right to act without retreating.

The evidence amply sustains the verdict.

The judgment is affirmed.

---

## Statford v. State, 50 Fla. 134 (1905)

Willie Stafford was convicted of manslaughter, and brings error. Affirmed.

### Syllabus by the Court

In a prosecution for homicide, instructions asked by the defendant on the subject of self-defense, which do not include the proposition that the defendant, to justify his acts on the ground of self-defense, must have used all reasonable means within his power and consistent with his own safety to avoid danger and to avert the necessity of taking the life of the deceased-a limitation which has been approved by this court in several cases-are properly refused when the charge given by the court as to self-defense was full and correct under the facts of the case.

In the prosecution of Willie Stafford for homicide, where the acts of the participants at the beginning of the fatal encounter are shown in evidence by eyewitnesses without material variance, and evidence of threats made by the deceased against the defendant eight days before the difficulty were admitted without objection, and not contradicted, other threats made by the deceased against 'one of the Staffords' more than fifteen months prior to the encounter were immaterial, and it was not error to exclude testimony as to such prior threats.

### Opinion

The plaintiff in error was convicted of manslaughter in the circuit court for Holmes county, and to a judgment sentencing him to the state prison for seven years this writ of error was taken.

At the trial exception was taken to the refusal of the court to give each of three charges requested by the defendant, as follows:

'A person upon whom a felonious assault is made is not required to retreat in order to avoid taking the life of his assailant, but, if free from fault in bringing on the difficulty, he may stand his ground, and defend himself, even to the extent of taking life, if necessary to protect himself.'

'If the defendant was the aggressor in bringing on the difficulty originally, but afterward he honestly abandoned the difficulty, and withdrew, and Jones, knowing this, followed the defendant up, and assaulted him with a rail, likely to produce great bodily harm, the defendant was not required to retreat, but would be justified in standing his ground and defending himself, even to the extent of taking life, if necessary to protect himself.'

'If the defendant was not the aggressor in bringing on the difficulty in which Jones lost his life, and that Jones assaulted him (the defendant) with a rail, likely to produce great bodily harm, the defendant would be justified in standing his ground and defending himself, even to the extent of taking Jones' life.'

The refusal to give these charges cannot be said to be error under the facts of this case. They do not include the proposition that the defendant, to justify his acts on the ground of self-defense, must have used all reasonable means within his power and consistent with his own safety to avoid danger and to avert the necessity of taking the life of the deceased-a limitation which has *136 been approved by this court in several cases. Peaden v. State (Fla.) 35 South. 204; Snelling v. State (Fla.) 37 South. 917, the charge given by the court as to self-defense was quite full and correct, and covered the facts of the case.

Error is also assigned to the rejection by the court of evidence of threats made about 15 months before by the deceased against 'one of the Staffords,' which were not shown to have been communicated to the defendant. Where, as in this case, the acts of the participants at the beginning of the encounter are shown in evidence by eyewitnesses without material variance, and evidence of threats made by the deceased against the defendant eight days before the difficulty were admitted without objection, and not contradicted, other threats made by the deceased against 'one of the Staffords' more than fifteen months prior to the encounter were immaterial, and it was not error to exclude testimony as to such prior threats.

The evidence sustains the verdict.

The judgment is affirmed.

# CHAPTER 5

# THE FLORIDA CASTLE DOCTRINE

Florida case law discusses the exception to the common law duty to retreat "to the wall" when in one's residence, thus giving birth to Florida's own "Castle Doctrine" and removing the duty to retreat in one's home when facing an attack. In the case of *Pell v. State* 97 Fla. 650 (1929), the Court referenced prior court opinions from the 1800's which discussed the doctrine. Since its ruling in *Pell*, the Court has since issued numerous decisions regarding the development of the Castle Doctrine in Florida and has provided instances of expanded its privilege. The Court decisions continue the support the use of deadly force in defending oneself in his or her home so long as the deadly force was required to prevent death or great bodily harm.

Eventually the Court extended the Castle Doctrine in *Hedges v. State*, 172 So.2d 824 (Fla. 1965) and permitted the use of the defense when defending oneself against someone as a guest in the home. In *Hedges*, the two were in a long-term relationship but did not live together. At the time of the shooting, the decedent was an invitee in the home of the accused. The Court also reasoned that one's home is the "ultimate sanctuary."

But see *State v. Bobbitt*, 415 So.2d 724 (Fla. 1982), when the Court considered extending the Castle Doctrine to a co-occupant in the home. In *Bobbitt* the Court declined to extend the doctrine and reasoned that the accused spouse had an equal right to be in the home and that neither had the right to reject the other.

However, several years later, in *Weiand v. State*, 732 So.2d 1044 (Fla. 1999), the Court receded from its decision in *Bobbitt* and removed the duty to retreat in one's home even if the aggressor is a co-occupant or spouse of the accused. The Court discussed the potentially damaging effects of the prior decision and the refusal to abolish the duty to retreat in these circumstances, including victims of domestic violence.

In *State v. James*, 867 So.2d 414 (Fla. 3rdDCA 2003), the Third District Court of Appeals extended the Castle Doctrine further and allowed an employee the use of the Doctrine and removed his duty to retreat so long as the assailant was not a fellow employee. According the case, one could defend himself or herself at work without being required to retreat to the wall.

In 2005, the Florida legislator extended the Castle doctrine even further. The statute now provides for the Castle Doctrine to be applied to a persons home and occupied vehicle. Additionally, the statute created what is known now as the Florida Stand Your Ground Law and removed the common law duty to retreat altogether. The statute, in pertinent part, is as follows:

**776.013. Home protection; use or threatened use of deadly force; presumption of fear of death or great bodily harm**

(1) A person is presumed to have held a reasonable fear of imminent peril of death or great bodily harm to himself or herself or another when using or threatening to use defensive force that is intended or likely to cause death or great bodily harm to another if:

(a) The person against whom the defensive force was used or threatened was in the process of unlawfully and forcefully entering, or had unlawfully and forcibly entered, a dwelling, residence, or occupied vehicle, or if that person had removed or was attempting to remove another against that person's will from the dwelling, residence, or occupied vehicle; and

(b) The person who uses or threatens to use defensive force knew or had reason to believe that an unlawful and forcible entry or unlawful and forcible act was occurring or had occurred.

(2) The presumption set forth in subsection (1) does not apply if:

(a) The person against whom the defensive force is used or threatened has the right to be in or is a lawful resident of the dwelling, residence, or vehicle, such as an owner, lessee, or titleholder, and there is not an injunction for protection from domestic violence or a written pretrial supervision order of no contact against that person; or

(b) The person or persons sought to be removed is a child or grandchild, or is otherwise in the lawful custody or under the lawful guardianship of, the person against whom the defensive force is used or threatened; or

(c) The person who uses or threatens to use defensive force is engaged in a criminal activity or is using the dwelling, residence, or occupied vehicle to further a criminal activity; or

(d) The person against whom the defensive force is used or threatened is a law enforcement officer, as defined in s. 943.10(14), who enters or attempts to enter a dwelling, residence, or vehicle in the performance of his or her official duties and the officer identified himself or herself in accordance with any applicable law or the person using or threatening to use force knew or reasonably should have known that the person entering or attempting to enter was a law enforcement officer.

(3) A person who is attacked in his or her dwelling, residence, or vehicle has no duty to retreat and has the right to stand his or her ground and use or threaten to use force, including deadly force, if he or she uses or threatens to use force in accordance with s. 776.012(1) or (2) or s. 776.031(1) or (2).

(4) A person who unlawfully and by force enters or attempts to enter a person's dwelling, residence, or occupied vehicle is presumed to be doing so with the intent to commit an unlawful act involving force or violence.

(5) As used in this section, the term:

(a) "Dwelling" means a building or conveyance of any kind, including any attached porch, whether the building or conveyance is temporary or permanent, mobile or immobile, which has a roof over it, including a tent, and is designed to be occupied by people lodging therein at night.

(b) "Residence" means a dwelling in which a person resides either temporarily or permanently or is visiting as an invited guest.

(c) "Vehicle" means a conveyance of any kind, whether or not motorized, which is designed to transport people or property.

---

## Pell v. State, 97 Fla. 650 (1929)

Error to Circuit Court, Volusia County; M. G. Rowe, Judge.

Eddie Pell was convicted of murder in the second degree, and he brings error.

Reversed.

### Syllabus by the Court

Indictment for murder, charging that defendant with premeditated design to effect death killed certain person, held sufficient as against motion in arrest (Comp. Gen. Laws 1927, §§ 7137, 8368, 8369). Indictment for murder, as defined in Comp. Gen. Laws 1927, § 7137 (Rev. Gen. St. 1920, § 5035), charging that defendant on certain day 'unlawfully and with a premeditated design to effect death, did kill' certain person by shooting him with shotgun, held sufficient as against motion in arrest under sections 8368, 8369 (Rev. Gen. St. 1920, §§ 6063, 6064), though it might have been improved upon by specifically charging that premeditated design was to effect death of person killed.

Court's discussion not essential to decision is without force as precedent. That part of court's opinion which is not essential to decision of case is mere obiter dictum and without force as precedent.

Law presumes man intends to do what he actually does. In prosecution for crime, law presumes that man intends to do what he actually does.

On motion in arrest for defects in indictment, indictment should receive liberal construction. On motion in arrest for defects in indictments or informations, rule is that indictment should receive liberal construction, and that even informal or imperfect allegation of essential fact will be deemed sufficient.

In murder case, refusal to permit argument by defendant's counsel, relative to state's failure to have contents of barrel of deceased's pistol analyzed, held not error, in view of trial court's discretion. In prosecution for murder, refusal to permit argument by defendant's counsel as to state's failure to have contents of inside of barrel of deceased's pistol analyzed held not error, in view of discretion vested in trial judge, which is rarely abused, though it was opinion of reviewing court that such argument was not improper.

State's attorney must endeavor to get at real facts whether they lead to conviction or acquittal. State's attorney occupies semijudicial position, and it is his duty to endeavor to get at real facts whether they lead to conviction or acquittal.

Reversal will not be predicated on error in rulings on argument to jury, unless ruling is clearly prejudicial. Reversal will not be predicated on error in permitting or refusing to permit argument to jury, unless ruling is clearly erroneous and prejudicial, since mistake is inevitable now and then in making prompt ruling on border-line argument.

Search warrant not conforming strictly to statutory requirements is void. Search warrant must conform strictly to requirements of statute under which it is issued, or it is void.

In prosecution for murder of one making search under invalid warrant, such warrant, if admissible, called for instruction that it was admitted only to show deceased's purpose in entering defendant's premises (Comp. Gen. Laws 1927, § 8513). In prosecution for murder of officer attempting to search defendant's premises under search warrant not issued in duplicate, as required by Comp. Gen. Laws 1927, § 8513 (Acts 1923, c. 9321, § 11), such warrant, if admissible, called for instruction that it was admitted only to show purpose of deceased in going on defendant's premises, and not for showing any justification for such action.

In murder case, defendants having introduced evidence that deceased used profanity cannot object to state's rebuttal evidence that deceased did not profane language. In prosecution for murder, defendants, after having elicited testimony that deceased had been in habit of using profanity, held not in position to object to testimony of state's witnesses on rebuttal that deceased was not in habit of using profane language.

In prosecution for murder, which occurred on defendant's premises, self-defense charge should cover proposition that one assaulted on his own premises need not retreat. In prosecution for murder, in which difficulty occurred on defendant's own premises upon which deceased had entered under invalid search warrant, charge on self-defense should have covered proposition that person, if not aggressor, violently assaulted on his own premises, is not obliged to retreat in order to avoid difficulty, and may use such force as appears necessary to him as cautious and prudent man to save his life or save himself from grievous bodily harm.

## Opinion

*652 BROWN, J.

The writ of error in this case is to a judgment of the circuit court of Volusia county convicting the plaintiff in error of murder in the second degree. There was a motion in arrest of judgment in which the validity of the indictment was challenged. Murder in the first degree is defined by our statute in the following language:

'The unlawful killing of a human being, when perpetrated from a premeditated design to effect the death of the person killed or any human being, or when committed in the perpetration of or in the attempt to perpetrate any arson, rape, robbery or burglary, shall be murder in the first degree, and shall be punishable by death.' Section 7137, Comp. Gen. Laws; section 5035, Rev. Gen. Stats.

The indictment, eliminating the statement of venue and style of the case, was as follows:

'The Grand Jurors of the State of Florida, empaneled and sworn to inquire and true presentment make, in and for the body of the County of Volusia, upon their oaths do present, that Eddie Pell of the County of Volusia and State of Florida, on the 8th day of **112 July in the year of our Lord, One Thousand, Nine Hundred and Twenty-seven, in the County and State aforesaid, unlawfully and with a premeditated design to effect death, did kill D. E. Walker, by shooting him with a shot gun; and that the said Raymond Pell, with a premeditated design to effect death, was then and there present, aiding, abetting, comforting, procuring, encouraging, counselling and commanding the said Eddie Pell, the murder aforesaid, to do and commit, contrary to the form of the statute in such case made and provided, and against the peace and dignity of the State of Florida.'

*653 That part of the indictment in this case which charges Raymond Pell as a principal in the second degree, may be eliminated from consideration, as he was acquitted, and Eddie Pell, who was charged as principal in the first degree, and convicted, is the sole plaintiff in error here. Eliminating that portion applying to Raymond Pell, the indictment in this case follows quite closely the form suggested in the opinion in Reed v. State, 94 Fla. 32, 45, 113 So. 630, 635. While this suggestion was more or less apposite to the point being discussed, it was not essential to the decision in that case, and hence mere obiter dictum and without force as a precedent. However, inasmuch as the opinion in that case was concurred in by all the justices, without dissent, it is quite probable that the state attorney felt thereby justified in following the form of indictment therein suggested.

As against the objections made in the motion in arrest in this case, we think that the form of indictment used here was entirely sufficient, and constitutes a decided improvement over the ancient ponderous common-law form.

This form, as well as the one suggested in the Reed Case, might have been improved upon, and more meticulously accurate, if the charging part had read as follows:

'That Eddie Pell, on the 8th day of July, A. D. 1927, in the county and State aforesaid, unlawfully and from a premeditated design to effect the death of D. E. Walker, did kill said D. E. Walker by shooting him with a shot gun,' etc., but, for the reasons hereinafter given, we deem the indictment as written good as against a motion in arrest.

The contention of plaintiff in error, as we take it, is to the effect that this form is sufficient except in one particular, and that is the omission of the words, 'of said D. E. *654 Walker,' the person killed, after the words 'premeditated design to effect death.' But is not the meaning of the indictment perfectly plain, with these words omitted? We think so.
Under our statute, 'the unlawful killing of a human being, when perpetrated from a premeditated design to effect the death of the person killed or any human being,' is murder in the first degree.
The indictment in this case charged that the defendant, on a certain date and in the named county, 'unlawfully and with a premeditated design to effect death, did kill D. E. Walker, by shooting him with a shot gun-contrary to the form of the statute in such case made and provided,' etc.

The writer is disposed to think this indictment would have been sufficient as against the motion in arrest of judgment, even if the words, 'to effect death,' had been omitted, so that the charging part would have read: 'Unlawfully and with a premeditated design, did kill D. E. Walker by shooting him with a shot gun, contrary to the form of the statute,' etc. In either manner of statement there cannot possibly be any reasonable doubt, under the ordinary rules of legal and grammatical construction, as to just what the indictment charges and means. The law presumes that a man intends to do what he actually does. So, as the indictment charges that the defendant killed the deceased by shooting him with a gun, the presumption is that he intended to kill him, and not some other person or animal as has been contended. As the indictment charges that the defendant killed the deceased by shooting him with a gun, and that he killed him 'unlawfully and with a premeditated design to effect death,' this quoted clause must be construed in connection with the sentence as a whole, and so construed it means of course that he killed him with the intent to kill him, and from a premeditated design. Such an indictment certainly *655 charges every element of murder in the first degree, as defined by the short and simple, yet comprehensive and sufficient, definition prescribed by our statute, which, by the way, means practically the same thing as the common-law definition of murder, which is 'the unlawful killing of a human being with malice aforethought.' See Bird v. State, 18 Fla. 493.

Could the jury or the defendant have been misled by this indictment, or have mistaken its meaning? We think not. This form of indictment is much less likely to mislead or confuse than the archaic, cumbersome, and uselessly meticulous common-law form. Of course the old form is legally sufficient, as we have held in Daniels v. State, 52 Fla. 18, 41 So. 609, and several other cases, but, since we have adopted in this state a simple statutory definition of murder in the first degree, it is no longer necessary to use the old common-law form, with its unnecessarily detailed allegations, such as that the defendant then and there did make an assault with a certain gun then and there held in his hand, and then and there loaded with gunpowder and leaden bullets, and that he did then and there shoot off and discharge said gun at and upon the deceased, thereby and thus striking the body of said deceased with said leaden bullets, thereby inflicting on and in the body of said deceased one mortal wound, from which **113 said wound he did languish, and, languishing, died, etc. Such needless particularity of averment tends not only to confuse the mind, but also to produce variances in proof, in respect to matters which are really immaterial, as pointed out in the Reed Case, supra.

When we come down to the sensible use of plain everyday language, such as the man on the street (who often becomes the man on the jury) uses and understands, and such as is used in our statute defining the different degrees of homicide, and simply charge in an indictment that, in the county *656 and state aforesaid, 'A. B. unlawfully and from a premeditated design to effect the death of C. D., did kill C. D., by shooting him with a gun,' or cutting him with a knife, as the case may be, 'contrary to the form of the statute in such case made and provided and against the peace and dignity of the State of Florida,' we lose nothing of substance, pith, or dignity, while we gain much in directness, lucidity, and simplicity of statement, without omitting a single element of the crime charged.

Sections 6063 and 6064, Rev. Gen. Stats., now appearing as sections 8368 and 8369, Comp. Gen. Laws of 1927, read as follows:

6063. 'Every indictment shall be deemed and adjudged good which charges the crime substantially in the language of the statute prohibiting the crime or prescribing the punishment, if any such there be, or if at common law, so plainly that the nature of the offense charged may be easily understood by the jury.'

6064. 'No indictment shall be quashed or judgment arrested or new trial be granted on account of any defect in the form of the indictment, or of misjoinder of offenses or for any cause whatsoever, unless the court shall be of the opinion that the indictment is so vague, indistinct and indefinite as to mislead the accused and embarrass him in the preparation of his defense or expose him after conviction or acquittal to substantial danger of a new prosecution for the same offense.'

Under these statutes, this indictment is certainly sufficient, but it is probably good without them. Its brevity and conciseness, as compared with the old form, affords no just ground for criticism, so long as there is no sacrifice of certainty; that is, so long as every essential element of the *657 crime, as defined by the statute, is embraced in the indictment in plain, understandable language. No long or involved pleading is required of the defendant. Why require it of the state? The Constitution only requires that the 'nature and cause of the accusation' be stated. 'Fundamental reason,' says Bishop, 'constitutes the essence of all our rules of pleading; so that the only just change possible in them consists of the removal of excrescences which time and the carelessness of judicial practice have suffered to grow thereon.' 1 Bishop Crim. Prac. (2d Ed.) p. 277.

We are quite satisfied that everybody who read this indictment, including the court and jury and the defendant himself, knew just exactly what was intended to be charged as soon as they read it or heard it read. No objection was made to it until after the verdict. In Michael v. State, 40 Fla. 265, 23 So. 944, this court said:

'In an indictment for murder it is essentially necessary to set forth particularly the manner of the death, and the means by which it was effected, but in stating the facts which constitute the offense no technical terms are required, and an averment of the manner and means by which the deceased came to his death in concise and ordinary language and in such a way as to enable a person of common understanding to know what was intended, is sufficient.'

This court has frequently held that offenses defined by statute may be charged in the language of the statute, or in language of equivalent import; that it is not essential to follow the precise language of the statute, if its substance and meaning be charged.

Under the Alabama statute an indictment in the following language: 'The grand jury of said county charges that before the finding of this indictment' A. B. 'unlawfully, and *658 with malice aforethought, killed' W. R., 'by shooting him with a pistol, against the peace and dignity of the State of Alabama,' was held sufficient. Burton v. State, 141 Ala. 32, 37 So. 435.

If the reasoning of the contention here made against the validity of this indictment be applied to the time-honored common-law definition of murder, which is that 'murder is the unlawful killing of a human being with malice aforethought,' the accepted definition would have to be held insufficient, because it does not read: 'Murder is the unlawful killing of a human being with malice aforethought against the human being killed.' Yet this overparticularity of statement is not only unnecessary, but would lead to a certain degree of inaccuracy, as a general definition, for it is well settled in this as well as other jurisdictions that one who kills one person, while attempting and intending with premeditated design (or malice aforethought ) to kill another person, is guilty of murder in the first degree.

Upon motions in arrest of judgment for alleged defects in indictments or informations, the rule, announced in many decisions of this court, is that the indictment should receive a liberal construction, and that even an informal or imperfect allegation of an essential fact will be deemed a sufficient averment of that fact. Smith v. State, 72 Fla. 449, 73 So. 354.

For these reasons we think the court below was justified in overruling the motion in arrest of judgment.

Plaintiff in error was convicted of murder **114 in the second degree and given a life sentence. The evidence shows that plaintiff in error, together with his brother, Raymond Pell, were proceeding in the former's automobile to their home in Osteen and met D. E. Walker on the street, passing him without salutations from either. Arriving at home, the Pell brothers lodged the car in the garage, Walker proceeding *659 to a store opposite Pell's home. Eddie Pell went in to his house and was eating his midday meal when he was called by some one to the rear of the house. He went out, unarmed according to the testimony for the defense, but with a gun according to a witness for the state, and found Walker in his garage, undertaking to make a search thereof and engaged in an altercation with his brother Raymond. It appears from Raymond's testimony that Walker had stated that he had a search warrant and had been asked by Raymond to let him read it, which request was refused; the refusal being accompanied by voluble profanity and a blow in the face which knocked Raymond through the side door of the garage. This was seen by Eddie Pell, who remonstrated, and that Walker, cursing him and threatening to kill him, raised his pistol to shoot Eddie, who, undertaking to dodge the bullet from the pistol, came within reach of an automatic shot gun, which was in the garage, with which he shot and killed Walker, firing two or three shots in quick succession into his body. He then went to the house of a nearby deputy sheriff and gave himself up.

There was evidence to the effect that a pistol such as he, an officer, usually carried, with certain chambers empty, was found near the hand of the deceased, lying in blood and sand according to the defendant's witnesses, but lying in clean sand according to testimony adduced by the state, and that an exploded shell of the same kind as those in the pistol was afterward found nearby. There was also evidence that some months prior to this fatal encounter Walker had endeavored to search plaintiff in error's car and had fired several shots at him and his brother, or the car, as they were leaving the scene, one of which struck the fender. There was also testimony showing threats by Walker against Pell, and by Pell against Walker. The state introduced considerable evidence as to the physical conditions at the scene *660 of the homicide, and the position of the wounds on the body of the deceased, evidently for the purpose of showing that one of the shots entered from the rear, and to rebut the defendant's testimony mony as to how the killing took place. The state also produced testimony that the pistol of the deceased had rust in the barrel and no odor of powder about it, as tending to show that it had not been recently fired; that, if the pistol had been fired, it would have cleaned the barrel and left it free of rust. The defendant contended that the pistol had been lying in blood and sand after the deceased fell, and it was this which had given the appearance of rust in the barrel. In this connection, there was evidence that the defendant's counsel, at the preliminary hearing, had requested a witness for the state to remove, by use of a clean handkerchief, some of the substance attached to the inside of the barrel so that it could be examined and thus determine what it was, but that the request was not granted by the presiding magistrate.

During the course of the final argument in behalf of the defendant, his counsel, Mr. Thomas Palmer, sought to argue to the jury that, inasmuch as the automatic pistol filed in evidence in the case had been in the custody of the state ever since the preliminary hearing, it was the duty of the state to have had the contents of the inside of the barrel analyzed, and that, by reason of the revolver having been in the custody of the state, the defendants had not had the contents analyzed for the benefit of the defendants. To this line of argument, the state attorney objected, which objection was sustained by the court, and the court directed Mr. Palmer not to proceed with that line of argument to the jury. To this ruling, defendants excepted, and same is assigned as error.

Under the circumstances shown by the evidence in this case, in making this argument, counsel was, in our opinion, *661 within the bounds of that considerable degree of latitude which is allowed counsel in argument. And this, too, without any necessary reflection upon the state attorney. The evidence of the state's witnesses, which he no doubt fully accepted, was to the effect that the pistol had been found lying in clean sand, and he therefore doubtless was satisfied in his own mind that the substance in the barrel was necessarily rust, and not blood, and that no microscopic examination was necessary. If he had had any doubt about it, he should, and no doubt would, have had the examination and test made. The state attorney, as we have said, occupies a semijudicial position, and it is his duty to endeavor to get at the real facts whether they lead to conviction or acquittal. But on the other hand, there was evidence for the defendant that the pistol had been lying in blood and sand, and counsel for defendant had therefore some ground to infer and believe that the substance in the barrel was blood that flowed into it after the shooting, and that the state, in whose custody it was, should have had it analyzed. The sincerity of counsel's belief was indicated by his request for examination at the preliminary trial. The language used by defendant's counsel in his endeavor to present this argument was not unparliamentary and did not indicate that it sprang from any animus toward, or desire to case any reflection upon, the state's counsel. The state, having the **115 closing argument, might have said in reply that, under the circumstances, it became the duty of the defendant to make formal application to the state attorney or to the court for an analysis by some qualified person of the substance in question, before making any criticism of the state's counsel for failure to have it done; that the state's testimony showed such an examination to be unnecessary in the opinion of counsel for the state, and hence no duty to have it done existed. Thus the court might without error have permitted *662 this argument, leaving it to counsel for the state to reply to the same in their closing argument. Yet we are not convinced that the court erred in not permitting it. A considerable degree of discretion is vested in our nisi prius judges in this matter of the arguments of counsel, and it is a discretion which is rarely abused; and, when it is, it is usually on the side of leniency and liberality as to the scope thereof, rather than that of too great a strictness. Counsel should usually be permitted to argue all reasonable inferences which may be drawn from the evidence, or any part thereof, but the due administration of justice requires that our trial judges should exercise with firmness their power and duty to keep the scope and character of argument within proper bounds, and their efforts to do so are to be commended rather than criticized. See Henderson v. State, 94 Fla. 318, 113 So. 689; Johnson v. State, 88 Fla. 461, 102 So. 549. It is sometimes a very delicate and difficult duty to perform. Objections to such arguments, like the one here in question, which might be said to fall within 'the twilight zone,' must be ruled upon promptly, and a mistake is inevitable now and then, but, unless the ruling of the trial judge is clearly erroneous and prejudicial, reversal should not be predicated thereon.

As shown by the evidence, the search warrant was not made out and issued in duplicate, as required by the statute, section 11 of chapter 9321, Acts of 1923, now appearing as section 8513, Comp. Gen. Laws. Only one copy was made and issued. The statute requires that: 'All search warrants issued shall be in duplicate, and said duplicate shall be delivered to the officer with the original warrant, and when the officer serves the warrant he shall deliver a copy to the person named in the warrant, or in his absence, to some person in charge of, or living on the premises,' etc. The warrant must conform strictly to the requirements of the statute under which it is issued, otherwise it is void. 35 Cyc. *663 1267; Gildrie v. State, 94 Fla. 134, 113 So. 704. And evidence obtained by a search under a warrant which fails to comply with the provisions of the statute is not admissible in evidence. Gildrie v. State, supra; Agnello v. U. S., 269 U. S. 20, 46 S. Ct 4, 70 L. Ed. 145, 51 A. L. R. 409. 'When searches and seizures are made pursuant to the command of a search warrant both the search warrant and the prerequisite oath or affirmation required for it must conform strictly to the constitutional and statutory provisions authorizing their issue. This is true because there is no process known to the law the execution of which is more distressing to the citizen or that actuates such intense feeling of resentment on account of its humiliating and degrading consequences.' Jackson v. State, 87 Fla. 262, 99 So. 548.

When the search warrant which was found in the pocket of the deceased was offered in evidence by the state while making out its case in chief, the court sustained the defendant's objection to its admission. But the defendant's testimony showed that the deceased had said he had a search warrant, and later, in the course of the state's testimony in rebuttal, the state attorney again offered in evidence the search warrant, 'which,' he stated, 'accounts for the mission upon which the dead man was at the time of the shooting.' The defendant again objected upon the ground that it had been proven that the warrant had not been issued as required by the statute; also upon the ground 'that the offer is unlimited, and if offered at all at this stage of the trial, the purpose for which it is offered must be set forth.' The objection was overruled, and the warrant admitted without comment by the court, and read in evidence. Nor was anything said about it by the court in instructing the jury. We think that in this action the court was in error. If the illegal search warrant was admissible at all, and we are inclined to think that it was, when admitting it the court *664 should have instructed the jury to the effect that it was admitted in evidence only for whatever light it might shed upon the mission or purpose of the deceased in going upon the defendant's premises, but not for the purpose of showing any legal justification for such action, or for any attempted search of the premises, on the part of the deceased. The brief statement made by the state attorney when offering the search warrant the second time was not sufficient to dispense with explicit instructions by the court to the jury, confining their consideration of it strictly to the purpose for which it was admitted. Without such instructions the jury might well have concluded that the court considered the search warrant legal and admissible generally, and sufficient to justify the deceased in his attempted search of the defendant's garage.

Testimony of several witnesses in behalf of the state on rebuttal was admitted to the effect that the deceased was not in the habit of using profane language. Some of this testimony was admitted without objection by the defendants, but some of it was **116 objected to. Aside from the abstract question as to the admissibility vel non of such evidence [Wigmore Evid. (2d Ed.) §§ 92-99, 375 et seq.], the defendants were not in a position to object, as they had let down the bars by eliciting testimony from witness Brooks (page 513 of the transcript) that the deceased had been in the habit of using profanity.

The charge of the court, on the subject of self-defense, closed with these words: 'And therefore the defendant, Eddie Pell, could not justify his acts as being in selfdefense, unless he used all reasonable means within his powers, consistent with his own safety, to avoid the danger and divert (avert) the necessity of killing the deceased, and you are to determine from

51

the evidence before you whether he used such reasonable means.'

*665 This charge was excepted to and assigned as error. It nowhere contained any qualification with reference to the defendant's duty to retreat. The charge was correct as far as it went (Doke v. State, 71 Fla. 633, 71 So. 917), but, under the evidence in the case, showing that the difficulty occurred on the defendant's own premises, upon which the deceased had entered for a purpose not authorized by law, the charge on this subject should have also covered the proposition that, if a person is not the aggressor in a difficulty, and is violently assaulted on his own premises, he is not obliged to retreat in order to avoid the difficulty, but may stand his ground and use such force as may appear to him as a cautious and prudent man to be necessary to save his life or to save himself from grievous bodily harm.

This court, in Danford v. State, 53 Fla. 4, 43 So. 593, said:

'It cannot be denied that it is the duty of a party to avoid a difficulty which he has reason to believe is imminent, if he may do so without apparently exposing himself to death or great bodily harm (Stafford v. State, 50 Fla. 134, 39 So. 106; Snelling v. State, 49 Fla. 34, 37 So. 917; Peadon v. State 46 Fla. 124, text 135, 35 So. 204), and that whatever qualification this principle may in application have will defend upon the circumstances of each particular case. Allen v. United States, 164 U. S. 492, text 498, 17 S. Ct. 154 [41 L. Ed. 528]; Wharton on Homicide (2d Ed.) Sec. 485. For instance, a man violently assaulted in his own house or on his premises near his house is not obliged to retreat, but may stand his ground and use such force as may appear to him as a cautious and prudent man to be necessary to save his life or to save himself from great bodily harm. Allen v. United States, supra. A person whose life has been threatened is not obliged to quit his business *666 to avoid a difficulty. Ballard v. State, 31 Fla. 266, 12 So. 865. But he cannot lie in wait for his adversary. Smith v. State, 25 Fla. 517, 6 So. 482. In cases where a combat is mutually sought, the duty of retreating seems to apply to both parties, for both being in the wrong neither can right himself without retreating. I Bishop's New Cr. Law, Secs. 869, 870.'
See, also, Graham v. State, 98 Ohio St. 77, 120 N. E. 232, 18 A. L. R. 1272; Beard v. U. S., 158 U. S. 550, 15 S. Ct. 962, 39 L. Ed. 1087.

The right to stand one's ground without retreating when violently assaulted in his own home or on his own premises, in a difficulty which he did not provoke, should form an element of the instructions on the law of self-defense in cases where there is evidence tending to show such state of facts. People v. Hecker, 109 Cal. 451, 42 P. 307, 30 L. R. A. 403, 409.

The first and second requested charges for the defendant dealt somewhat with this question of the defendant's being upon his own premises, in connection also with the subject of threats by the deceased, and apparent necessity to take life in self-defense, but, as they omitted the element of freedom from fault in bringing on the difficulty, or of the defendant not being the aggressor, there was no error in their refusal. The other requested charges were covered by the court's general charge.

For the errors pointed out, the judgment must be reversed.

Reversed.

. . . .

## Hedges v. State, 172 So.2d 824 (Fla. 1965)

Decision quashed and cause remanded.

### Opinion

THORNAL, Justice.

By a petition for a writ of certiorari we have for review a decision of a District Court of Appeal which allegedly conflicts with prior decisions of this Court and another District Court of Appeal.

We must decide whether a charge deferring degrees of homicide, including manslaughter, should likewise include a definition of excusable and justifiable homicide.

The facts are revealed by the opinion of the District Court of Appeal. Hedges v. State, 165 So.2d 213. The petitioner Hedges was indicted for the first degree murder of her paramour. She was convicted of manslaughter. The trial judge initially instructed the jury on all degrees of unlawful homicide. He also instructed on justifiable and excusable homicide. After deliberating some six hours and recessing for the night a juror advised the court:

'We would like for you to go over the different degrees that were stated the other day. There is some confusion as to the different charges there.'

In response to the juror's request, the judge repeated his charge on the degrees of unlawful homicide. However, he denied a request of petitioner's attorney to include his charge on justifiable and excusable homicide. The judge had the view that since the jury requested only the charges on degrees of homicide, he had no obligation to repeat his charge on justifiable and excusable homicide. Petitioner's attorney pointed out that the statute which defines manslaughter specifically excludes justifiable and excusable homicide. He contended that it would be impossible to define manslaughter accurately without reference to the other two types of homicide. The District Court affirmed the ruling of the trial judge. Its decision is now here for review.

Petitioner claims that the decision below conflicts with the prior decision of this Court in Tipton v. State, 97 So.2d 277, and, the decision of the Court of Appeal, First District, in Bagley v. State, 119 So.2d 400.

In Tipton we held that the manslaughter statute, Section 782.07, Florida Statutes, F.S.A., necessarily requires a definition of excusable homicide as an essential of a complete charge. In Bagley the First District held that an instruction should be complete. It should cover every essential element of the offense charged. There the information charged second degree murder but in his instructions the trial judge omitted a part of the statutory definition of justifiable homicide. This resulted in a reversal.

In the instant case the trial judge deemed it unnecessary to define justifiable and excusable homicide in order to inform the jury correctly on the several degrees of unlawful homicide, including manslaughter.

An examination of the cases cited, as well as others which we shall mention, leads us to a jurisdictional conflict of decisions and hence a consideration of the merits.

*826 Section 782.07, Florida Statutes, F.S.A., defines Manslaughter as follows:

'The killing of a human being by the act, procurement or culpable negligence of another, in cases where such killing shall not be justifiable or excusable homicide nor murder * * * shall be deemed manslaughter * * *.'

One notes immediately that it is in the nature of a residual offense. If a homicide is either justifiable or excusable it cannot be manslaughter. Consequently, in any given situation, if an act results in a homicide that is either justifiable or excusable as defined by statute, a not guilty verdict necessarily ensues. The result is that in order to supply a complete definition of manslaughter as a degree of unlawful homicide it is necessary to include also a definition of the exclusions. A definition of the higher degrees of homicide-as one of the manslaughter exclusions-would be necessary only if a higher degree is charged, as was the case here.

We have already mentioned Tipton v. State, supra, and Bagley v. State, supra. There are other decisions which underscore the presence of jurisdictional conflict and support the conclusion which we here reach.

It will be recalled that the instant problem arose when the trial judge repeated-at jury request-his instructions on degrees of homicide. It is proper for a judge to limit the repetition to the charges requested. Hysler v. State, 85 Fla. 153, 95 So. 573. However, the repeated charges should be complete on the subject involved. The giving of a partial instruction fails to inform the jury fully and often leads to undue emphasis on the part given as against the part omitted. McCray v. State, 89 Fla. 65, 102 So. 831. The McCray decision is particularly persuasive. There the judge repeated certain charges on the degrees of homicide and failed to add that, if the evidence warranted, the defendant could be convicted of any of the degrees 'or be acquitted'. The failure to add the possibility of acquittal was held error.

In Graives v. State, 127 Fla. 182, 172 So. 716, a manslaughter case, we held that it is the duty of the judge to instruct on justifiable and excusable homicide. In Halfrich v. State, 122 Fla. 375, 165 So. 286, we held that it is always proper to instruct on justifiable and excusable homicide when defining manslaughter as a degree of unlawful homicide. The reason given was to enable the jury to understand the definition of manslaughter.

In the instant case when the judge repeated his charges on degrees of homicide he should have included the requested definitions of justifiable and excusable homicide. Failure to do so erroneously left with the jury an incomplete, and, potentially misleading instruction. Bagley v. State, supra; McCray v. State, supra.

Having taken jurisdiction we should dispose of another point raised by the petitioner. It is contended that when instructing on the law of self-defense, the judge should have informed the jury that if attacked in her own home the accused is not obliged to retreat in order to avoid the difficulty. The state replies that the 'home rule exception' to the requirement of retreat is not available when, as here, the attacker does not enter as a trespasser. Moreover, contends the state, there was no need for an instruction on retreat because the evidence showed no duty of the accused to retreat.

We think the last contention of the state would be sound here but for the actual instruction on self-defense given by the judge. As we read it from the state's brief it contained the following:
'In order to justify the taking of human life, the accused must have used all reasonable means within his power and consistent with his own safety to avoid the danger and avert the necessity of taking human life.'

The instruction correctly stated the law as far as it went but again it was *827 not complete. The quoted language placed upon the accused the duty to use all reasonable means consistent with her own safety to avoid the danger and avert the necessity of taking human life. To the lay mind this well could be construed to mean the duty to run or to get out of the way. There is no such duty when one is assaulted in his own home, despite the common law duty to 'retreat to the wall' when one is attacked elsewhere. Pell v. State, 97 Fla. 650, 122 So. 110. While Pell involved a trespasser, it clearly states the rule to be that when one is violently assaulted in his own house or immediately surrounding premises, he is not obliged to retreat but may stand his ground and use such force as prudence and caution would dictate as necessary to avoid death or great bodily harm. When in his home he has 'retreated to the wall'. Pell further decides that such an instruction should be an element of the charge on self-defense where the evidence supports it. Other courts have held that a man is under no duty to retreat when attacked in his own home. His home is his ultimate sanctuary. Wharton's Criminal Law and Procedure (Anderson), Vol. 1 p. 519; People v. Newcomer, 118 Cal. 263, 50 P. 405, State v. Grantham, 224 S.C. 41, 77 S.E.2d 291, State v. Bissonnette, 83 Conn. 261, 76 A. 288. In view of the charge actually given, we find that the rule of non-necessity of retreat in one's own home should have been included.

The petitioner will be entitled to a new trial.

The decision under review is quashed and the cause is remanded to the Court of Appeal, Second District, for disposition consistent herewith.

It is so ordered.

## State v. Bobbitt, 415 So.2d 724 (Fla. 1982)

Defendant was convicted in the Circuit Court, Duval County, Ralph W. Nimmons, J., of manslaughter of her husband. New trial was granted and State appealed. The District Court of Appeal, First District, 389 So.2d 1094, held that evidence did not support the manslaughter conviction in view of plea of self-defense, and reversed conviction and remanded with directions to discharge defendant. On application for review, the Supreme Court, Alderman, J., held that privilege not to retreat, premised on maxim that everyman's home is his castle which he is entitled to protect from invasion, did not apply where both defendant and her husband had equal rights to be in the "castle" and neither had legal right to eject the other.

Decision of district court quashed and remanded for further proceedings consistent with opinion.

Overton, J., dissented and filed opinion in which Boyd, J., concurred.

### Opinion

ALDERMAN, Justice.

We have for review the decision of the District Court of Appeal, First District, in State v. Bobbitt, 389 So.2d 1094 (Fla. 1st DCA 1980), holding that the "castle doctrine" or privilege of nonretreat in the home applies even where co-occupants, both legally residing in the home, are involved. This decision expressly and directly conflicts with the Fourth District's decision in Conner v. State, 361 So.2d 774 (Fla. 4th DCA 1978), cert. denied, 368 So.2d 1364 (Fla.1979), holding that where the assailant and the victim are both legal occupants of the same home, the privilege of nonretreat does not apply and the defense-of-the-home instruction need not be given. We agree with the Fourth District and hold that when an assailant and the victim are legal occupants of the same home, the "castle doctrine" does not apply. We therefore quash the decision of the First District.

*725 Elsie Bobbitt was charged with second-degree murder of her husband and was found guilty by a jury of manslaughter. Her husband, who was legally residing with her, attacked her in their home without provocation, and she shot him. She moved for a new trial on the basis that the trial court erroneously failed to instruct the jury that one unlawfully attacked in her own home has no duty to retreat. The instruction she requested provided: One unlawfully attacked in his own home or on his own premises has no duty to retreat and may lawfully stand his ground and meet force with force, including deadly force, if necessary to prevent imminent death or great bodily harm to himself or another, or to prevent the commission of a forcible felony.

The trial court did instruct the jury as follows on the duty to retreat prior to the use of deadly force:
If attacked by another, even though the attack is wrongful, he has the legal duty to retreat if by doing so he can avoid the necessity of using deadly force without increasing his own danger, but a person placed in a position of imminent danger of death or great bodily harm to himself by the wrongful attack of another has no duty to retreat if to do so would increase his own danger of death or great bodily harm.

Agreeing with Bobbitt that it had reversibly erred in failing to give her requested instruction as to the privilege of nonretreat, the trial court granted her motion for new trial.

The State appealed to the First District Court of Appeal and contended that the requested instruction on the exception to duty to retreat did not apply because the victim was not an intruder. Placing much reliance on our decision in Hedges v. State, 172 So.2d 824 (Fla.1965), the district court disagreed and held that the law did not require that respondent retreat when attacked in her home prior to acting in self-defense and that the jury should have been instructed that Bobbitt had no duty to retreat. It decided that the privilege of nonretreat applies regardless of whether legal co-occupants or intruders are involved. Having determined that there was no duty on the part of Bobbitt to retreat and, therefore, that any finding by the jury regarding failure to retreat was irrelevant, the First District considered in this light whether, as a matter of law, the evidence supported the manslaughter conviction in view of Bobbitt's plea of self-defense. It held that it did not, and it reversed the conviction and remanded with directions to discharge Bobbitt.

In our early decision of Pell v. State, 97 Fla. 650, 122 So. 110 (1929), we held that where one is not the aggressor and is violently assaulted on his own premises by a trespasser, he is not obliged to retreat but may stand his ground and use such force as necessary to save his life or to save himself from great bodily harm. Quoting from our earlier decision of Danford v. State, 53 Fla. 4, 43 So. 593 (1907), we said:

"It cannot be denied that it is the duty of a party to avoid a difficulty which he has reason to believe is imminent, if he may do so without apparently exposing himself to death or great bodily harm (Stafford v. State, 50 Fla. 134, 39 So. 106; Snelling v. State, 49 Fla. 34, 37 So. 917; Peadon v. State, 46 Fla. 124, text 135, 35 So. 204), and that whatever qualification this principle may in application have will depend upon the circumstances of each particular case. Allen v. United States, 164 U.S. 492, text 498, 17 S.Ct. 154 [41 L.Ed. 528]; Wharton on Homicide (2d Ed.) Sec. 485. For instance, a man violently assaulted in his own house or on his premises near his house is not obliged to retreat, but may stand his ground and use such force as may appear to him as a cautious and prudent man to be necessary to save his life or to save himself from great bodily harm. Allen v. United States, supra. A person whose life has been threatened is not obliged to quit his business to avoid a difficulty. Ballard v. State, 31 Fla. 266, 12 So. 865. But he cannot lie in wait for his adversary. Smith v. State, 25 Fla. 517, 6 So. 482. In cases where a combat is mutually sought, *726 the duty of retreating seems to apply to both parties, for both being in the wrong neither can right himself without retreating. I Bishop's New Cr. Law, Secs. 869, 870."

Pell v. State, 122 So. at 116.

Much later in Hedges v. State, we concluded that there was no duty to retreat on the part of the defendant who, while in her home, was attacked by her paramour. Up until the time of the attack the paramour had been an invitee on the premises, not a legal co-occupant of the premises. Thereafter, his initial lawful presence in Hedges' home was rendered unlawful by his assault upon her. We rejected the State's contention that the privilege of nonretreat in the home is not available when the attacker "does not enter as a trespasser." 172 So.2d at 826 (emphasis added). We were not, however, confronted with nor did we resolve the question now presented for our resolution.

Although in Watkins v. State, 197 So.2d 312 (Fla. 4th DCA 1967), the Fourth District decided that the trial court had erred in refusing to charge the jury on the doctrine of non-necessity of retreat where the defendant killed her common-law husband in the dwelling in which they both resided, it later expressly receded from this expanded version of the castle doctrine in Conner v. State. The emphasis in Conner is on the sanctity of human life. The Fourth District noted that in its original applications, the castle doctrine had in view only attacks from external aggressors. We agree with the following rationale expressed by Judge Letts, speaking for the Fourth District in Conner :
[W]e see no reason why a mother should not retreat from her son, even in her own kitchen. Such a view does not render her defenseless against a member of her family gone berserk, because the instruction on retreat ...

concludes, "but a person placed in a position of imminent danger of death or great bodily harm to himself by the wrongful attack of another has no duty to retreat if to do so would increase his own danger of death or great bodily harm."

361 So.2d at 776.

We hold that the privilege not to retreat, premised on the maxim that every man's home is his castle which he is entitled to protect from invasion, does not apply here where both Bobbitt and her husband had equal rights to be in the "castle" and neither had the legal right to eject the other. As Judge Letts pointed out in Conner, this holding does not leave an occupant of a home defenseless against the attacks of another legal co-occupant of the premises since "a person placed in imminent danger of death or great bodily harm to himself by the wrongful attack of another has no duty to retreat if to do so would increase his own danger of death or great bodily harm." Fla.Std.Jury Instr. (Crim.), 2d ed., p. 64. This instruction was properly given the jury in the present case.

Accordingly, we quash the decision of the district court and remand for further proceedings consistent with this opinion.

It is so ordered.

SUNDBERG, C. J., and ADKINS and McDONALD, JJ., concur.
OVERTON, J., dissents with an opinion, in which BOYD, J., concurs.
OVERTON, Justice, dissenting.

I strongly dissent. The majority opinion holds that a wife who claims that she killed her husband in self-defense in the home is not entitled to a jury instruction that she had no duty to retreat under the castle doctrine. At the same time, the opinion recognizes that the opposite is true for a woman who claims that she killed her paramour in self-defense, whom she had invited into her home, reaffirming that she is entitled to the castle doctrine jury instruction and that she had no duty to retreat before using deadly force. The opinion distinguishes the two situations upon the basis that in the first situation the assailant is a cotenant and in the second the assailant is an invitee. I would treat cotenants, other family members, and invitees the same and *727 would hold, as to these types of antagonists, that one assailed in one's own home has only a limited duty to retreat.

Present law is clear that a person attacked in his home by an intruder has no duty to retreat and is entitled to the "castle doctrine"/no-duty-to-retreat jury instruction. Our current criminal standard jury instructions contain the following language regarding the issue of self-defense:

In deciding whether defendant was justified in the use of force likely to cause death or great bodily harm, you must judge [her] by the circumstances by which [she] was surrounded at the time the force was used. The danger facing the defendant need not have been actual; however, to justify the use of force likely to cause death or great bodily harm, the appearance of danger must have been so real that a reasonably cautious and prudent person under the same circumstances would have believed that the danger could be avoided only through the use of that force. Based upon appearances, the defendant must have actually believed that the danger was real.

The defendant cannot justify [her] use of force likely to cause death or great bodily harm unless [she] used every reasonable means within [her] power and consistent with [her] own safety to avoid the danger before resorting to that force.

The fact that the defendant was wrongfully attacked cannot justify [her] use of force likely to cause death or great bodily harm if by retreating [she] could have avoided the need to use that force. However, if the defendant was placed in a position of imminent danger of death or great bodily harm and it would have increased [her] own danger to retreat, then [her] use of force likely to cause death or great bodily harm was justifiable.

If the defendant was attacked in [her] own home or on [her] own premises, [she] had no duty to retreat and had the lawful right to stand [her] ground and meet force with force, even to the extent of using force likely to cause death or great bodily harm, if it was necessary to prevent death or great bodily harm to [herself] or another.

See Standard Jury Instruction 3.04(d) (emphasis supplied). The italicized portion of the above instruction embodies the so-called castle doctrine which the majority has ruled not applicable to respondent-wife in the instant case.

This Court has previously expressed the view that the castle doctrine is applicable when "the attacker does not enter as a trespasser" but is an invitee. Hedges v. State, 172 So.2d 824, 826 (Fla.1965). In Hedges, the woman defendant was attacked by her paramour, whom she had invited into her home. The instant majority opinion refuses to apply Hedges holding that, because the wife's assailant was her cotenant husband, she is not entitled to the castle doctrine instruction. This places the wife in the same position as if the altercation had occurred in a public place.

It has been a basic premise in our law that the home is a special place of protection and security. The castle doctrine emanated from this premise, and a majority of jurisdictions in this country have adopted the castle doctrine exception. In Rippie v. State, 404 So.2d 160, 161-62 (Fla. 2d DCA 1981), Judge Boardman set forth a historical background and legal basis for the doctrine, stating:

Many jurisdictions, including Florida, have expanded the "castle doctrine" to permit its use even when the attacker is not an intruder, Hedges v. State, 172 So.2d 824 (Fla.1965), and even when he is a co-occupant, Watkins v. State, 197 So.2d 312 (Fla. 4th DCA 1967). See also State v. Phillips, 38 Del. 24, 187 A. 721 (1936); State v. Leeper, 199 Iowa 432, 200 N.W. 732 (1924); People v. Tomlins, 213 N.Y. 240, 107 N.E. 496 (1914); State v. McPherson, 114 Minn. 498, 131 N.W. 645 (1911); Thomas v. State, 583 S.W.2d 32 (Ark.1979); State v. Browning, 28 N.C.App. 376, 221 S.E.2d 375 (1976); People v. Garrett, 82 Mich.App. 178, 266 N.W.2d 458 (1978); State v. Grantham, 224 S.C. 41, 77 S.E.2d 291 (1953); Ison v. State, 252 Ala. 25, 39 So.2d 249 (1949). Judge *728 Cardozo in the Tomlins case stated his reasoning as follows:

It is not now and never has been the law that a man assailed in his own dwelling is bound to retreat. If assailed there, he may stand his ground and resist the attack. He is under no duty to take to the fields and the highways, a fugitive from his own home. More than 200 years ago it was said by Lord Chief Justice Hale (1 Hale's Pleas of the Crown, 486): In case a man "is assailed in his own house, he need not flee as far as he can, as in other cases of se defendendo, for he hath the protection of his house to excuse him from flying, as that would be to give up the protection of his house to his adversary by flight." Flight is for sanctuary and shelter, and shelter, if not sanctuary, is in the home.

107 N.E. at 497. And in Jones v. State, 76 Ala. 8, 14 (1884), it was aptly inquired: " 'Why ... should one retreat from his own house, when assailed by a partner or cotenant, any more than when assailed by a stranger who is lawfully upon the premises? Whither shall he flee, and how far, and when may he be permitted to return?' "

The Conner court [361 So.2d 774 (Fla. 4th DCA 1978), cert. denied, 368 So.2d 1364 (Fla.1979) ], however, chose to recede from the expanded version of the "castle doctrine" it had espoused in Watkins and held that "where both the antagonist and the assailed are legal occupants of the same 'castle,' neither one having the legal right to eject the other, the defense of home instruction need not be given." Conner, supra, at 776. A few other jurisdictions are in accord with Conner. See State v. Crawford, 66 W.Va. 114, 66 S.E. 110 (1909); State v. Grierson, 96 N.H. 36, 69 A.2d 851 (1949); State v. Lamb, 134 N.J.Super. 575, 342 A.2d 533, aff'd, 71 N.J. 545, 366 A.2d 981 (1976); Commonwealth v. Walker, 447 Pa. 146, 288 A.2d 741 (1972).

(Emphasis supplied.) The Second District Court of Appeal in Rippie rejected the Fourth District Court of Appeal's decision in Conner but did not fully embrace the castle doctrine. It held that, where the assailant is a cotenant in the home, there should be a limited duty to retreat. The Second District held that such a duty should not, however, mandate that the person assailed must retreat from the dwelling house proper. I agree. The Second District's solution is more reasonable than the illogical distinction between a cotenant and an invitee adopted by the majority.

Under the majority opinion, a woman killing her paramour in her home has more protection under the law than a woman who kills her husband in her home. More difficult still to understand is the application of the majority's rule to the situation where a mother is attacked in her home by a nineteen-year-old son. If the son is living in the home, the mother has a duty to retreat before she can use deadly force, but, if the son is not residing in the home, the mother has no duty to retreat before such force is used. This result and the majority's rule is in fact a minority position which does not recognize the realities of life.

Human life is precious, and deadly combat should be avoided if at all possible when imminent danger to oneself can be avoided. A limited duty to retreat, however, as suggested by the Second District Court of Appeal in Rippie, is, I think, an appropriate middle ground that recognizes both the duty to retreat and the sanctity of the home. To achieve this purpose, I would adopt an additional jury instruction when the assailant in one's home is an invitee, a cotenant, or a family member, to provide as follows:
If the defendant was attacked in [his/her] own home, or on [his/her] own premises, by a cotenant, family member, or invitee, [he/she] has a duty to retreat to the extent reasonably possible but is not required to flee [his/her] home and has the lawful right to stand [his/her] ground and meet force with force even to the extent of using force likely to cause death or great bodily harm if it was necessary to prevent death or great bodily harm to [himself/herself] or another.

*729 This instruction would cure the artificial legal distinctions and disparate results created by the majority decision.

In disposing of the instant case, I would find that Hedges was the law at the time of the trial for invitees and cotenants and that it should have controlled. I agree with the trial judge and a unanimous district court of appeal that respondent was entitled to the castle doctrine instruction and should have a new trial. I would approve the district court decision and direct the use of the suggested limited duty-to-retreat jury instruction in the retrial.

BOYD, J., concurs.

---

## Weiand v. State, 732 So.2d 1044 (1999)

Defendant's conviction of second-degree murder with a firearm for shooting husband was affirmed by the District Court of Appeal, 701 So.2d 562, and on rehearing the question of right to nonretreat jury instruction was certified. The Supreme Court, Pariente, J., held that: (1) as a matter of first impression, there is no duty to retreat from the residence before a defendant may justifiably resort to deadly force in self-defense against a co-occupant, if that force is necessary to prevent death or great bodily harm, receding from State v. Bobbitt, 415 So.2d 724; (2) omission of jury instruction on privilege of nonretreat was not cured by general self-defense instruction that retreat is not required if it would increase danger of death or great bodily harm; (3) privilege of nonretreat instruction is equally available to all those lawfully residing in the premises, receding from Hedges v. State, 172 So.2d 824; and (4) improper exclusion of eyewitness testimony to corroborate defendant's assertion of prior abuse by husband was not harmless error.

District Court of Appeal decision quashed.

Wells, J., concurred in part and dissented in part with an opinion, in which Shaw, J., concurred.

**Opinion**

PARIENTE, J.

We have for review a decision of the Second District Court of Appeal certifying the following question to be of great public importance:

SHOULD THE RULE OF STATE V. BOBBITT, 415 So.2d 724 (Fla. 1982), *1047 BE CHANGED TO ALLOW THE CASTLE DOCTRINE INSTRUCTION IN CASES WHERE THE DEFENDANT RELIES ON BATTERED-SPOUSE SYNDROME EVIDENCE (AS NOW AUTHORIZED BY STATE V. HICKSON, 630 So.2d 172 (Fla. 1994)[) ] TO SUPPORT A CLAIM OF SELF-DEFENSE AGAINST AN AGGRESSOR WHO WAS A COHABITANT OF THE RESIDENCE WHERE THE INCIDENT OCCURRED?
Weiand v. State, No. 95-01121, on rehearing from 701 So.2d 562 (Fla. 2d DCA 1997).

We rephrase the question as follows:

SHOULD THE LAW IMPOSE A DUTY TO RETREAT FROM THE RESIDENCE BEFORE A DEFENDANT MAY JUSTIFIABLY RESORT TO DEADLY FORCE IN SELF-DEFENSE AGAINST A CO-OCCUPANT, IF THAT FORCE IS NECESSARY TO PREVENT DEATH OR GREAT BODILY HARM?

As rephrased, we answer the certified question in the negative and recede from our contrary holding in Bobbitt.

....

## II. FACTS

Kathleen Weiand was charged with first-degree murder for the 1994 shooting death of her husband Todd Weiand. Weiand shot her husband during a violent argument in the apartment where the two were living together with their seven-week-old daughter. At trial Weiand claimed self-defense and presented battered spouse syndrome3 evidence pursuant to Hickson in support of her claim. Weiand testified that her husband had beaten and choked her throughout the course of their three-year relationship and had threatened further violence if she left him.

Two experts, including Dr. Lenore Walker, a nationally recognized expert on battered women, testified that Weiand suffered from "battered woman's syndrome." Dr. Walker detailed Weiand's history of abuse by her husband and testified about the effect of the abusive relationship on Weiand. Based on her studies, her work with Weiand and Weiand's history of abuse, Dr. Walker concluded that when Weiand shot her husband she believed that he was going to seriously hurt or kill her.

Dr. Walker opined that there were several reasons why Weiand did not leave the apartment that night during the argument, despite apparent opportunities to do so: she felt that she was unable to leave because she had just given birth seven weeks earlier; she had been choked unconscious; she was paralyzed with terror; and experience had taught her that threats of leaving only made her husband more violent.

At the charge conference following the close of the evidence, defense counsel requested that the following standard jury instruction be given:
If the defendant was attacked in [his][her] own home or on [his][her] own premises, [he][she] had no duty to retreat and had the lawful right to stand [his][her] ground and meet force with force, even to the extent of using force likely to cause death or great bodily harm if it was necessary to prevent either death or great bodily harm.

Fla. Std. Jury Instr. (Crim.), "Justifiable Use of Deadly Force," § 3.04(d), at 49 (brackets in original). In accordance with this Court's opinion in Bobbitt, the trial court refused the request to give this "defense of home" instruction. Instead, the trial court only gave the instruction applicable in all self-defense cases regarding the duty to retreat:
The fact that the defendant was wrongfully attacked cannot justify her use of force likely to cause death or great bodily harm if by retreating she could have avoided the need to use that force.

See Fla. Std. Jury Instr. (Crim.), "Justifiable Use of Deadly Force," § 3.04(d), at 48.

During closing arguments, the prosecutor used this standard instruction to the State's advantage by emphasizing Weiand's duty to retreat. The prosecutor stressed as "critical" that the killing could not be considered justifiable homicide unless Weiand had exhausted every reasonable means to escape the danger, including fleeing her home:
She had to exhaust every reasonable means of escape prior to killing him. Did she do that? No. Did she use the *1049 phone that was two feet away? No. Did she go out the door where her baby was sitting next to? No. Did she get in the car that she had driven all over town drinking and boozing it up all day? No.

The jury found Weiand guilty of second-degree murder and the trial court sentenced her to eighteen years' imprisonment. The Second District affirmed her conviction and sentence, see Weiand, 701 So.2d at 565, but on rehearing certified the question of whether this Court should recede from Bobbitt.

## III. THE PRIVILEGE OF NONRETREAT FROM THE RESIDENCE

Under Florida statutory and common law, a person may use deadly force in self-defense if he or she reasonably believes that deadly force is necessary to prevent imminent death or great bodily harm. See § 776.012, Fla. Stat. (1995); Wilson v. State, 30 Fla. 234, 255, 11 So. 556, 561 (1892); DeLuge v. State, 710 So.2d 83, 84 (Fla. 5th DCA 1998); Fla. Std. Jury Instr. (Crim.) § 3.04(d), at 46. Even under those circumstances, however, a person may not resort to deadly force without first using every reasonable means within his or her power to avoid the danger, including retreat. See Bobbitt, 415 So.2d at 725; Hedges v. State, 172 So.2d 824, 827 (Fla.1965). The duty to retreat emanates from common law, rather than from our statutes. See Hedges, 172 So.2d at 827.4

There is an exception to this common law duty to retreat "to the wall," which applies when an individual claims self-defense in his or her own residence. See id. at 827; Pell v. State, 97 Fla. 650, 665, 122 So. 110, 116 (1929); Danford v. State, 53 Fla. 4, 13, 43 So. 593, 597 (1907). An individual is not required to retreat from the residence before resorting to deadly force in self-defense, so long as the deadly force is necessary to prevent death or great bodily harm. See Hedges, 172 So.2d at 827; Pell, 97 Fla. at 665, 122 So. at 116; Danford, 53 Fla. at 13, 43 So. at 597.

The privilege of nonretreat from the home, part of the "castle doctrine,"5 has early common law origins. See Bobbitt, 415 So.2d at 725; Hedges, 172 So.2d at 827; Pell, 97 Fla. at 665, 122 So. at 116; Danford, 53 Fla. at 13, 43 So. at 597; New York v. Tomlins, 213 N.Y. 240, 107 N.E. 496, 497-98 (1914). In Tomlins, the defendant claimed self-defense when attacked in his home by his son. 107 N.E. at 496. In reversing the defendant's conviction because the duty to retreat instruction was given, Justice Cardozo explained the historical basis of the privilege of nonretreat from the home:

It is not now and never has been the law that a man assailed in his own dwelling is bound to retreat. If assailed there, he may stand his ground and resist the attack. He is under no duty to take to the fields and the highways, a fugitive from his own home. More than 200 years ago it was said by Lord Chief Justice Hale: In case a man "is assailed *1050 in his own house, he need not flee as far as he can, as in other cases of se defendendo, [[[[6] for he hath the protection of his house to excuse him from flying, as that

would be to give up the protection of his house to his adversary by flight." Flight is for sanctuary and shelter, and shelter, if not sanctuary, is in the home.... The rule is the same whether the attack proceeds from some other occupant or from an intruder.
Id. at 497-98 (emphasis supplied) (citations omitted).

In Hedges, this Court applied the privilege of nonretreat from the residence where the attacker was not an intruder but an invitee with the defendant's permission to be on the premises. In that case, the defendant and the victim had maintained a long-term intimate relationship, and on the morning of the shooting the victim was an invitee, lawfully in the defendant's home. See Hedges v. State, 165 So.2d 213, 214-15 (Fla. 2d DCA 1964), quashed, 172 So.2d 824 (Fla.1965). In instructing the jury on the law of self-defense, the trial court informed the jury that the defendant was required to use "all reasonable means within his power and consistent with his own safety to avoid the danger and avert the necessity of taking human life." Hedges, 172 So.2d at 826. The trial court failed to instruct the jury that the defendant was under no duty to retreat from her residence. See id. at 827.

In reversing the conviction of manslaughter, our Court held:

The instruction correctly stated the law as far as it went but again it was not complete. The quoted language placed upon the accused the duty to use all reasonable means consistent with her own safety to avoid the danger and avert the necessity of taking human life. To the lay mind this well could be construed to mean the duty to run or to get out of the way. There is no such duty when one is assaulted in his own home, despite the common law duty to "retreat to the wall" when one is attacked elsewhere. Pell v. State, 97 Fla. 650, 122 So. 110 [ (1929) ]. While Pell involved a trespasser, it clearly states the rule to be that when one is violently assaulted in his own house or immediately surrounding premises, he is not obliged to retreat but may stand his ground and use such force as prudence and caution would dictate as necessary to avoid death or great bodily harm. When in his home he has "retreated to the wall." Pell further decides that such an instruction should be an element of the charge on self-defense where the evidence supports it. Other courts have held that a man is under no duty to retreat when attacked in his own home. His home is his ultimate sanctuary.
Id. at 826-27 (emphasis supplied).

Eighteen years later, in Bobbitt, this Court considered whether the privilege of nonretreat from the home should also apply where the defendant killed her co-occupant husband in self-defense, after being attacked without provocation. 415 So.2d at 725-26. This Court rejected the extension of

Hedges7 under those circumstances:

[T]he privilege not to retreat, premised on the maxim that every man's home is his castle which he is entitled to protect from invasion, does not apply here where both Bobbitt and her husband had equal rights to be in the "castle" and neither had the legal right to eject the other.
Id. at 726.

Justice Overton, in a strongly-worded dissent, disagreed with the majority's decision because it was contrary to a "basic *1051 premise in our law that the home is a special place of protection and security." Id. at 727. He further criticized the distinction made by the majority that authorized the privilege of nonretreat instruction in cases like Hedges, where the aggressor was an invitee with a legal right to be on the premises, but not where the aggressor was a co-occupant. See id. at 726-27.

At the time we rendered our decision in Bobbitt in 1982, we were in a minority of jurisdictions8 that refused to extend the privilege of nonretreat from the residence where the aggressor was a co-occupant. Since our decision in Bobbitt, an even greater number of jurisdictions have declined to impose a duty to retreat from the residence.9 See generally H.J. Alperin, Annotation, Homicide: Duty to Retreat Where Assailant and Assailed Share the Same Living Quarters, 26 A.L.R.3d 1296 (1969 & Supp.1998).

## IV. RECONSIDERATION OF OUR DECISION IN BOBBITT

We now conclude that it is appropriate to recede from Bobbitt and adopt Justice Overton's well-reasoned dissent in that case. We join the majority of jurisdictions that do not impose a duty to retreat from the residence when a defendant uses deadly force in self-defense, if that force is necessary to prevent death or great bodily harm from a co-occupant.

There are two distinct reasons for our conclusion. First, we can no longer agree with Bobbitt 's minority view that relies on concepts of property law and possessory rights to impose a duty to retreat from the residence. 415 So.2d at 726. Second, based on our increased understanding of the plight of victims of domestic violence in the years since our decision in Bobbitt, we find that there are sound policy reasons for not imposing a duty to retreat from the residence when a defendant resorts to deadly force in self-defense against a co-occupant. The more recent decisions of state supreme courts confronting this issue have recognized that imposing a duty to retreat from the residence has a potentially damaging effect on victims of domestic violence claiming self-defense. See, e.g., New Jersey v. *1052 Gartland, 149

N.J. 456, 694 A.2d 564, 569-71 (1997); Ohio v. Thomas, 77 Ohio St.3d 323, 673 N.E.2d 1339, 1343 (1997).


## A. Bobbitt's Possessory Rights Distinction

In refusing to extend the privilege of nonretreat in Bobbitt, we held that
the privilege not to retreat ... does not apply here where both Bobbitt and
her husband had equal rights to be in the "castle" and neither had the legal
right to eject the other.
415 So.2d at 726. Thus, our decision in Bobbitt appears to have been
grounded upon the sanctity of property and possessory rights, rather than
the sanctity of human life.

In light of our decision in Hedges, our holding in Bobbitt created a
distinction that resulted in the privilege of nonretreat applying when the
defendant is defending herself against an invitee, with a legal right to be on
the premises, but not when defending herself against a co-occupant, who
also had a legal right to be on the premises. Justice Overton illustrated the
effect of this "illogical distinction" in his dissenting opinion in Bobbitt:
Under the majority opinion, a woman killing her paramour in her home has
more protection under the law than a woman who kills her husband in her
home. More difficult still to understand is the application of the majority's
rule to the situation where a mother is attacked in her home by a nineteen-
year-old son. If the son is living in the home, the mother has a duty to
retreat before she can use deadly force, but, if the son is not residing in the
home, the mother has no duty to retreat before such force is used.
Id. at 728.

Bobbitt 's distinction based on possessory rights may be important in the
context of defending the home. See supra note 6; Falco v. State, 407 So.2d
203, 208 (Fla.1981); Alday v. State, 57 So.2d 333, 333 (Fla.1952); State v.
White, 642 So.2d 842, 844 (Fla. 4th DCA 1994). However, the privilege of
nonretreat from the home stems not from the sanctity of property rights,
but from the time-honored principle that the home is the ultimate
sanctuary. See Hedges, 172 So.2d at 827; Tomlins, 107 N.E. at 497-98. As
has been asked rhetorically, if the duty to retreat from the home is applied
to a defendant attacked by a co-occupant in the home, "whither shall he
flee, and how far, and when may he be permitted to return?" Jones v.
Alabama, 76 Ala. 8, 16 (1884); see also Gartland, 694 A.2d at 570.

The omission of the jury instruction on the privilege of nonretreat from the
home is not cured by the jury instruction given in all self-defense cases that

there is no legal duty to retreat if retreating would increase the danger of death or great bodily harm. See Fla. Std. Jury Instr. (Crim.), "Justifiable Use of Deadly Force," § 3.04(d) at 48. In Hedges, the jury was instructed that the defendant had to use all reasonable means consistent with her own safety to avoid the danger before resorting to deadly force in self-defense. 172 So.2d at 826-27. We found that the instructions were incomplete because, without the privilege of nonretreat instruction, the jury may have believed that the defendant had a duty to retreat from her home. See id. at 827. For the same reason, we find that in circumstances where the nonretreat instruction is applicable, the instructions are incomplete and misleading if the nonretreat instruction is not given. See id.

## B. Implications for victims of domestic violence

1. Imposing a duty to retreat from the home may adversely impact victims of domestic violence.

Although the State argues that nothing has changed in the intervening years since Bobbitt to require us to recede from that decision, to the contrary, much has changed in the public policy of this State, *1053 based on increased knowledge about the plight of domestic violence victims. It is now widely recognized that domestic violence "attacks are often repeated over time, and escape from the home is rarely possible without the threat of great personal violence or death." Thomas, 673 N.E.2d at 1343. As quoted by the New Jersey Supreme Court:
Imposition of the duty to retreat on a battered woman who finds herself the target of a unilateral, unprovoked attack in her own home is inherently unfair. During repeated instances of past abuse, she has "retreated," only to be caught, dragged back inside, and severely beaten again. If she manages to escape, other hurdles confront her. Where will she go if she has no money, no transportation, and if her children are left behind in the "care" of an enraged man?
....
What [the duty to retreat] exception means for a battered woman is that as long as it is a stranger who attacks her in her home, she has a right to fight back and labors under no duty to retreat. If the attacker is her husband or live-in partner, however, she must retreat. The threat of death or serious bodily injury may be just as real (and, statistically, is more real) when her husband or partner attacks her in home, but still she must retreat.
Gartland, 694 A.2d at 570-71 (quoting Maryanne E. Kampmann, The Legal Victimization of Battered Women, 15 Women's Rts. L. Rep. 101, 112-113 (1993)).

Studies show that women who retreat from the residence when attacked by their co-occupant spouse or boyfriend may, in fact, increase the danger of harm to themselves due to the possibility of attack after separation. According to Dr. Lenore Walker, "[t]he batterer would often rather kill, or die himself, than separate from the battered woman." Lenore E. Walker, Terrifying Love: Why Battered Women Kill and How Society Responds 65 (1989).

Experts in the field explain that separation or retreat can be the most dangerous time in the relationship for the victims of domestic violence because "[v]iolence increases dramatically when a woman leaves an abusive relationship." Executive Office of the Governor, The Governor's Task Force on Domestic Violence, The First Report at 55 (January 31, 1994) (hereinafter First Report ). A leading expert in the field cites one study which revealed that forty-five percent of the murders of women "were generated by the man's 'rage over the actual or impending estrangement from his partner.' " Donald G. Dutton, The Batterer: A Psychological Profile 15 (1995). Another study found that the murder of the battered victim was often "triggered by a walkout, a demand, a threat of separation [which] were taken by the men to represent intolerable desertion, rejection and abandonment. Thus ... the threat of separation is usually the trigger for violence." Kampman, supra at 104 (brackets in original).

The imposition of a duty to retreat from one's residence when faced with a violent aggressor has the most significant impact on women because an overwhelming majority of victims of domestic violence are women. According to the statistics compiled by the Governor's Task Force on Domestic Violence, seventy-three percent of domestic violence victims are women. See First Report, supra at 47; Executive Office of the Governor, The Governor's Task Force on Domestic and Sexual Violence, The Third Report at Appendix S (March 31, 1997) (hereinafter Third Report ). Domestic violence is the single major cause of injury to women, more frequent than auto accidents, rapes, and muggings combined. See First report, supra at 2. "Over four thousand women die annually at the hands of their abuser," id. at 3, and in 1995, of all female homicide victims, thirty-nine percent were killed during domestic violence incidents. See *1054 Third report, supra at Appendix S.10 These studies and other similar findings in the intervening years since Bobbitt provide proof of Justice Overton's observation that retaining a duty to retreat from the home "clearly penalizes spouses, and particularly wives, in defending themselves from an aggressor spouse." State v. Rippie, 419 So.2d 1087, 1087 (Fla.1982) (Overton, J., dissenting).

2. A jury instruction on the duty to retreat may reinforce common myths about domestic violence.

There is a common myth that the victims of domestic violence are free to leave the battering relationship any time they wish to do so, and that the " 'beatings' could not have been too bad for if they had been, she certainly would have left." State v. Kelly, 97 N.J. 178, 478 A.2d 364, 377 (1984). See also Joan H. Krause, Of Merciful Justice and Justified Mercy: Commuting the Sentences of Battered Women who Kill, 46 Fla. L.Rev. 699, 712 (1994).

This stereotypical view may extend beyond the jurors deciding the case. One commentator quotes a Maryland judge expressing disbelief of the defendant's claimed defense:
The reason I don't believe it is because I don't believe anything like this could happen to me. If I was you and someone had threatened me with a gun, there is no way that I could continue to stay with them.
Martha R. Mahoney, Victimization or Oppression? Women's Lives, Violence and Agency, in The Public Nature of Private Violence 59, 73 (Martha A. Fineman & Roxanne Mykituk eds.1994) (quoting a Maryland Judge quoted in Maryland's Gender Bias in the Courts Report (Murphy 1993)).

A jury instruction placing a duty to retreat from the home on the defendant may serve to legitimize the common myth and allow prosecutors to capitalize upon it. The prosecutor capitalized on the jury instruction and the common myth in this case when she questioned the believability of Weiand's claims and asked the jury why Weiand did not "go out the door?" and why she did not "get in the car?" before resorting to violence. See also Krause, supra at 712.

In Hickson we authorized the admission of battered spouse syndrome evidence to rebut the common myths concerning battered women and explained the very real dangers faced by women in these relationships. Hickson, 630 So.2d at 174; see Kelly, 478 A.2d at 377. As the expert evidence demonstrates, there are many reasons battered women do not feel free to leave a battering relationship. The woman might have been isolated from her family by the abuser, she may not be able to afford to go, or she may realize that leaving is more dangerous than staying. See Kampman, supra at 101; see generally Hickson, 630 So.2d at 174. To re-affirm Bobbitt with its duty to retreat from the home would undermine our reasons in Hickson for approving expert testimony on battered woman's syndrome.

## C. The Evolution of Public Policy

In tandem with the increased understanding of domestic violence, there has been a substantial evolution in the public policy of this state since Bobbitt.11 A decision *1055 to recede from Bobbitt at this time is an evolution of the common law consistent with this evolution in public policy.12

Developments in all three branches of government since Bobbitt reflect the public's concern regarding the plight of victims of domestic violence. For example, recognizing that "violence against women in their own homes is epidemic in our society," First Report, supra at 3, the executive branch has established a task force on domestic violence, whose purpose is the issuance of reports and recommendations which document "the extent of our awareness, and the responsiveness of our resources to battered women and their families." First Report, supra at v.

Since the Bobbitt decision, the Legislature has enacted numerous laws in response to the plight of the victims of domestic violence.13 For example, the law now requires that a person arrested for domestic violence must be held until first appearance, and the court must consider the safety of the victim in determining whether the defendant should be released and in setting the defendant's bail. See § 741.2901(3), Fla. Stat. (1997); ch. 95-195, § 3, at 1763, Laws of Fla. In addition, the provisions relating to domestic violence injunctions have been substantially revised. The injunctive relief that the trial court can now grant includes awarding the petitioner the exclusive use and possession of the dwelling the parties share. See § 741.30(6)(a) 2., Fla. Stat. (1997); ch. 84-343, § 10, at 1989, Laws of Florida. The legislature has made it illegal for any person under a final domestic injunction to possess a weapon. See § 741.30(6)(f), Fla. Stat. (1998). Law enforcement officers investigating alleged incidents of domestic violence are now required to notify the victim about the various resources of protection and the steps to take in pursuing prosecution. See § 741.29(1), Fla. Stat. (1997); ch. 84-343, § 12, at 1991, Laws of Fla.14

*1056 Likewise, since our decision in Bobbitt, the judiciary has focused judicial resources on the plight of victims of spousal abuse. Eight domestic violence courts have been organized within the twenty judicial circuits of Florida. See Office of the State Courts Administrator, Survey of the Circuits (Sept.1997) (on file with the State Court Adm'r, Fla. Sup.Ct.). As of 1997, more than half of the twenty judicial circuits had domestic violence task forces. See Third Report, supra at 12. To further the goal of proper judicial response to incidents of domestic violence, this Court has been active in providing educational opportunities for judges throughout the state, and circuit and county court judges now have training available specifically addressing domestic violence and its related issues. See Office of the State Courts Administrator, The Florida Supreme Court's Annual Report to the Florida Legislature on Activities Conducted Under the Court Education Trust Fund at attachment IV (Oct. 8, 1998) (on file with State Court Adm'r, Fla. Sup.Ct.).

## D. The Jury Instruction on the Privilege of Nonretreat

The public policy of this State is clearly directed at reducing domestic violence. We have thus considered the views of jurists in the minority position, who have expressed a concern that eliminating a duty to retreat from the residence will increase violence because "[t]here are dramatically more opportunities for deadly violence in the domestic setting than in the intrusion setting." Thomas, 673 N.E.2d at 1347 (Pfeifer, J., dissenting); see also Bobbitt, 415 So.2d at 726; Conner v. State, 361 So.2d 774, 776 (Fla. 4th DCA 1978).

While there may be more opportunities for violence in the domestic setting, no empirical data has been presented, either through expert testimony or studies, demonstrating any correlation between eliminating a duty to retreat from the home and an increase in incidents of domestic violence. In contrast, a duty to retreat from the home adversely affects victims of domestic violence by placing them at greater risk of death or great bodily harm. In addition, failing to inform the jurors that the defendant had no duty to retreat from the residence when attacked by a co-occupant may actually reinforce commonly held myths concerning domestic violence victims.

As Florida's Standard Jury Instructions on self-defense make clear, a defendant is entitled to resort to deadly force in self-defense only if that force is necessary to protect himself or herself from death or great bodily harm. See Hedges, 172 So.2d at 827; Pell, 97 Fla. at 665, 122 So. at 116; Danford, 53 Fla. at 13, 43 So. at 597; Fla. Std. Jury Instr. (Crim.), "Justifiable Use of Deadly Force," § 3.04(d), at 46-48. Furthermore, the jury is instructed in all cases-even those cases where the privilege of nonretreat instruction is given-that:

The defendant cannot justify the use of force likely to cause death or great bodily harm unless [he][she] used every reasonable means within [his] [her] power and consistent with [his][her] own safety to avoid the danger before resorting to that force.

Id. at 48; Hedges, 172 So.2d at 827. Thus, the availability of the nonretreat instruction does not "invite" violence.

Nonetheless, we conclude that Justice Overton's "middle ground" instruction, as set forth in his dissent in Bobbitt, 415 So.2d at 728, satisfies any concern that eliminating a duty to retreat might invite violence. This instruction imposes a limited duty to retreat within the residence to the extent reasonably possible, but no duty to flee the residence. Accordingly, we adopt the following instruction:15

*1057 If the defendant was attacked in [his/her] own home, or on [his/her] own premises, by a co-occupant [or any other person lawfully on the premises] [he/she] had a duty to retreat to the extent reasonably possible without increasing [his/her] own danger of death or great bodily harm. However, the defendant was not required to flee [his/her] home and had the lawful right to stand [his/her] ground and meet force with force even to the extent of using force likely to cause death or great bodily harm if it was necessary to prevent death or great bodily harm to [himself/herself].

See id.; see also Rippie v. State, 404 So.2d 160, 162 (Fla. 2d DCA 1981), quashed 419 So.2d 1087 (Fla.1982).

It is our increased knowledge of the complexities of domestic violence that provides the impetus for reconsidering our decision in Bobbitt. However, in deciding whether the privilege of nonretreat instruction is available we consider it inappropriate to distinguish between victims of domestic violence and other defendants who have been attacked by a co-occupant in the residence. This was the position espoused in Justice Overton's dissent. See Bobbitt, 415 So.2d at 728.

As Justice Kogan stated in his concurring opinion in Perkins v. State, 576 So.2d 1310, 1314 (Fla.1991), "[t]he right to fend off an unprovoked and deadly attack is nothing less than the right to life itself, which [article I, section 2] of our Constitution declares to be a basic right." Thus, the privilege of nonretreat instruction should be equally available to all those lawfully residing in the premises, provided, of course, that the use of deadly force was necessary to prevent death or great bodily harm.16 Because this instruction will apply to both invitees and co-occupants alike, we recede from Hedges to the extent that Hedges does not require a middle-ground instruction for invitees.

. . . .

## VI. CONCLUSION

In conclusion, we hold that there is no duty to retreat from the residence before resorting to deadly force against a co-occupant or invitee if necessary to prevent death or great bodily harm, although there is a limited duty to retreat within the residence to the extent reasonably possible. Thus, we answer the certified question, as rephrased, in the negative, recede from Bobbitt, recede in part from Hedges, and adopt the middle-ground jury instruction proposed by Justice Overton in his dissent in Bobbitt.

This opinion and the instruction will be applicable in all future cases, and all cases that are pending on direct review, or not yet final. See State v. Gray, 654 So.2d 552, 554 (Fla.1995). This opinion will not, however, apply retroactively to convictions that have become final. See State v. Glenn, 558 So.2d 4, 6 (1990); see generally Witt v. State, 387 So.2d 922, 928-29 (Fla.1980). The decision of the Second District is quashed.

It is so ordered.

HARDING, C.J., ANSTEAD, J., and OVERTON and KOGAN, Senior Justices, concur.
WELLS, J., concurs in part and dissents in part with an opinion, in which SHAW, J., concurs.
WELLS, J., concurring in part and dissenting in part.

---

## State v. James, 867 So.2d 414 (Fla. 2003)

Petition granted; order quashed; case remanded.

### Opinion

GREEN, J.

The State of Florida has brought this petition for issuance of a writ of certiorari seeking to quash an order of the trial court determining that the respondent/defendant, Alexander James, is entitled to utilize a "castle doctrine" defense and concomitant jury instruction at his upcoming trial for second degree murder. At issue is whether James, who was a social guest or visitor in the home of another at the time of his alleged commission of second degree murder, is entitled to the "castle doctrine" privilege and jury instruction. We conclude that he is not and for the reasons which follow, grant the petition and quash the circuit court's order under review.

Respondent James had been acquainted with a woman named Semantha Beall for approximately one week before he came to her apartment on the morning of April 17, 1997. The respondent had been to Beal's apartment once before to assist her in putting together a bed frame. The respondent and Beal had agreed that on April 17 they would travel together from Beal's apartment to the residence of Beal's mother so that James could perform some electrical work there. When James arrived at Beal's apartment, Beal answered the door wearing a black negligee and invited him inside. They engaged in consensual sex and later showered together.

Shortly thereafter, the victim, Larry Ferguson, Beal's allegedly abusive ex-boyfriend, showed up at Beal's apartment. Beal went to the front door and told the victim to leave because she had a boyfriend in her apartment. Beal and the respondent thereafter got dressed to leave.

As Beal and the respondent were exiting the apartment, they spotted the victim who was still waiting outside. The victim grabbed Beal and began to choke her. The respondent intervened to prevent the victim from hurting her. The three ended *416 up back in the apartment. Once there, the respondent and the victim continued to struggle and Beal was able to flee her apartment to telephone for help.2

During the struggle between the respondent and the victim, a gun and the victim's cellular telephone fell to the floor. The respondent picked up the gun and the victim fled into the bedroom. Beal testified during her deposition that as she was running back to her apartment, she saw the respondent standing in the entrance door to the apartment with his back facing her. The respondent extended his right arm up in front of himself and fired a shot through the partially closed bedroom door. The bullet hit the victim in the chest at a downward angle. The victim died a few days later and the respondent was charged with second degree murder.

Prior to jury selection, the state moved in limine to prevent the respondent from arguing that he had no duty to retreat from the apartment prior to resorting to deadly force under the "castle doctrine." The trial court denied the motion, ruling that the respondent, as a guest or invitee, had a greater right to be in the apartment than the victim as a trespasser.3 The state now seeks the issuance of a writ of certiorari quashing this order. We grant the petition.

Both Florida statutory and common law permit the use of deadly force in self-defense if a person reasonably believes that such force is necessary to prevent imminent death or great bodily harm. Weiand v. State, 732 So.2d 1044, 1049 (Fla.1999). Specifically, section 776.012, Florida Statutes (1995), provides that "a person ... is justified in the use of deadly force only if he reasonably believes that such force is necessary to prevent imminent death or great bodily harm to himself or another or to prevent the imminent commission of a forcible felony." Even under these circumstances, there is still a Florida common law duty to use every reasonable means to avoid the danger, including retreat, prior to using deadly force. Weiand, 732 So.2d at 1049.

The "duty to retreat" rule has an exception, known as the "castle doctrine," which espouses that one is not required to retreat from one's residence, or one's "castle," before using deadly force in self-defense, so long as the deadly force is necessary to prevent death or great bodily harm. Id. Florida courts have defined the castle doctrine as a privilege one enjoys in one's own dwelling place. The Florida Supreme Court has said:

when one is violently assaulted in his own house or immediately surrounding premises, he is not obliged to retreat but may stand his ground and use such force as prudence and caution would dictate as necessary to avoid death or great bodily harm. When in his home he has "retreated to the wall." ... [A] man is under no duty to retreat when attacked in his own home. His home is his ultimate sanctuary.

Id. at 1050 (quoting Hedges v. State, 172 So.2d 824, 827 (Fla.1965)). See also Alday v. State, 57 So.2d 333, 333 (Fla.1952) ("The law authorizes one whose home is assaulted without lawful authority to use such force as is necessary to repel the assailant." *417 ); Russell v. State, 61 Fla. 50, 54 So. 360, 361 (1911) ("One attacked in his home need not retreat, and he may use all necessary force to eject the intruder, whom he may kill in doing it, if this extreme measure appears unavoidable."); but see Williamson v. State, 101 Fla. 1219, 133 So. 109, 110 (1931)(denying castle doctrine protection to defendant for homicide committed in residence from which defendant had moved). The castle doctrine privilege of non-retreat is "equally available to all those lawfully residing in the premises, provided, of course, that the use of deadly force was necessary to prevent death or great bodily harm." Weiand, 732 So.2d at 1057.

We have further extended the "castle doctrine" privilege to employees in their place of employment, while lawfully engaged in their occupations. See

Redondo v. State, 380 So.2d 1107, 1108 (Fla. 3d DCA 1980)(finding employee of convenience store entitled to non-retreat instruction when attacked at his place of business); State v. Smith, 376 So.2d 261 (Fla. 3d DCA 1979) (holding manager of store not obligated to retreat when attacked in or immediately adjacent to store). But see Frazier v. State, 681 So.2d 824, 825 (Fla. 2d DCA 1996)(agreeing that castle doctrine protects a worker in the workplace but making an exception where the aggressor was a co-worker). To date, this has been the only extension of the "castle doctrine" protection to a person not attacked in his or her own dwelling or residence.

The issue before us comes down to whether the castle doctrine privilege should be further extended to a temporary visitor or guest, since the respondent was not a resident of the apartment at the time of the alleged incident. We think that a further extension of the "castle doctrine" privilege to include a temporary social guest or visitor must be weighed against the underlying policy consideration of the "duty to retreat" rule as enunciated by Justice Overton's dissenting opinion in State v. Bobbitt, 415 So.2d 724, 728 (Fla.1982) (Overton, J., dissenting), and later adopted by the Supreme Court in Weiand, 732 So.2d at 1051: "[h]uman life is precious, and deadly combat should be avoided if at all possible when imminent danger to oneself can be avoided." Bobbitt, 415 So.2d at 728. Weiand, 732 So.2d at 1051. We believe that an overly broad extension of the castle doctrine would vitiate the retreat rule. The more places there are where one has castle doctrine protection, the fewer places there would be from which one has a duty to retreat. As the state insightfully observes, granting castle doctrine protection to a social guest or visitor would necessarily grant the guest or visitor innumerable castles wherever he or she is authorized to visit. That, in turn, would expand the privilege of non-retreat and encourage the use of deadly force. We agree and, therefore, decline to extend the "castle doctrine" privilege to a temporary social guest or visitor in the home of another.

The Florida Supreme Court has said that "the privilege of non-retreat from the home stems not from the sanctity of property rights, but from the time-honored principle that the home is the ultimate sanctuary." Weiand, 732 So.2d at 1052. In the instant case, although the respondent was temporarily present in the apartment with its owner's permission and had a right to be there as found by the trial court, this apartment could not, under the facts of this case, be deemed the respondent's ultimate sanctuary. Thus, given the respondent's status as a temporary social guest or visitor at the time of the alleged incident, he is not entitled to the use of a "castle doctrine" defense or jury instruction at his trial for second degree murder. *418 We therefore grant the petition and quash the order under review.

Petition for certiorari granted and case is remanded for further proceedings consistent with this opinion.

# CHAPTER 6

# FLORIDA'S STAND YOUR GROUND LAW

In 2005, the Florida Legislature abrogated the Common Law Duty to Retreat and enacted legislation known as the Stand Your Ground Law, which completely eliminated the duty to retreat. The law states that a person may use force, even deadly force, in certain circumstances.

The statute provides for the defense of person, the defense of property, and home protection (discussed earlier). Additionally, the Statute provides criminal and civil immunity.

### 776.012. Use or threatened use of force in defense of person

(1) A person is justified in using or threatening to use force, except deadly force, against another when and to the extent that the person reasonably believes that such conduct is necessary to defend himself or herself or another against the other's imminent use of unlawful force. A person who uses or threatens to use force in accordance with this subsection does not have a duty to retreat before using or threatening to use such force.

(2) A person is justified in using or threatening to use deadly force if he or she reasonably believes that using or threatening to use such force is necessary to prevent imminent death or great bodily harm to himself or herself or another or to prevent the imminent commission of a forcible felony. A person who uses or threatens to use deadly force in accordance with this subsection does not have a duty to retreat and has the right to stand his or her ground if the person using or threatening to use the deadly force is not engaged in a criminal activity and is in a place where he or she has a right to be.

## 776.031. Use or threatened use of force in defense of property

(1) A person is justified in using or threatening to use force, except deadly force, against another when and to the extent that the person reasonably believes that such conduct is necessary to prevent or terminate the other's trespass on, or other tortious or criminal interference with, either real property other than a dwelling or personal property, lawfully in his or her possession or in the possession of another who is a member of his or her immediate family or household or of a person whose property he or she has a legal duty to protect. A person who uses or threatens to use force in accordance with this subsection does not have a duty to retreat before using or threatening to use such force.

(2) A person is justified in using or threatening to use deadly force only if he or she reasonably believes that such conduct is necessary to prevent the imminent commission of a forcible felony. A person who uses or threatens to use deadly force in accordance with this subsection does not have a duty to retreat and has the right to stand his or her ground if the person using or threatening to use the deadly force is not engaged in a criminal activity and is in a place where he or she has a right to be.

## 776.032. Immunity from criminal prosecution and civil action for justifiable use or threatened use of force

(1) A person who uses or threatens to use force as permitted in s. 776.012, s. 776.013, or s. 776.031 is justified in such conduct and is immune from criminal prosecution and civil action for the use or threatened use of such force by the person, personal representative, or heirs of the person against whom the force was used or threatened, unless the person against whom force was used or threatened is a law enforcement officer, as defined in s. 943.10(14), who was acting in the performance of his or her official duties and the officer identified himself or herself in accordance with any applicable law or the person using or threatening to use force knew or reasonably should have known that the person was a law enforcement officer. As used in this subsection, the term "criminal prosecution" includes arresting, detaining in custody, and charging or prosecuting the defendant.

(2) A law enforcement agency may use standard procedures for investigating the use or threatened use of force as described in subsection (1), but the agency may not arrest the person for using or threatening to use force unless it determines that there is probable cause that the force that was used or threatened was unlawful.

(3) The court shall award reasonable attorney's fees, court costs, compensation for loss of income, and all expenses incurred by the defendant in defense of any civil action brought by a plaintiff if the court finds that the defendant is immune from prosecution as provided in subsection (1).

When a defendant files a motion notifying the Court of the Stand Your Ground immunity defense, the Court must conduct a pretrial evidentiary hearing to determine if the statutory immunity attaches to the defendant. In doing so, the Court must look at the "totality of the circumstances" leading up to the attack in question and review the appearance of the perceived danger in the eyes of a reasonably cautious and prudent person under similar circumstances and determine if such a person would have believed that the danger could only be avoided through the use of deadly force.[16]

This determination is also made from an *objective standard* rather than a *subjective standard*. This makes it irrelevant as to whether or not the defendant actually feared serious bodily injury or death. The objective standard shifts the focus on a fictitious reasonable prudent person in similar circumstances. Conversely, The subjective standard seeks to view the circumstances through the eyes of the subject.

In arguing immunity under the Stand Your Ground Law, the Defendant carries the burden of proof though he need only show this by a preponderance of the evidence. This is a relatively low legal threshold to meet and is less than the civil standard of clear and convincing evidence and much lower than the beyond a reasonable doubt burden in a criminal prosecution.[17]

The burden of proof is what the moving party must show, by testimony and other evidence, in order to be successful in the presentation of the claim or defense. The preponderance of evidence burden is not

---

[16] *Mobley v. State*, 132 So.3d 1160 (Fla. 3rd DCA, 2014)

[17] *Little v. State*, 111 So.3d 214 (Fla. 2nd DCA, 2013)

easily reduced to a simple formula and the quantum of evidence is not specific. However, to meet this burden of proof, one must present enough evidence to make the claim more likely than not. Put another way, over 50% likely. There are several types of burdens of proof depending on the type of legal matter. These include: preponderance of the evidence, clear and convincing, and beyond a reasonable doubt. The preponderance of the evidence is the lowest of these standards.

## Little v. State, 111 So.3d 214 (Fla. 2nd DCA, 2013)

Petition granted; conflict certified.

Northcutt, J., concurred, with opinion.

### Opinion

SILBERMAN, Chief Judge.

Aaron A. Little seeks certiorari review of the circuit court's order denying his motion to dismiss the criminal charge of second-degree murder with a firearm. Little argued that he shot the victim in self-defense and was entitled to immunity from criminal prosecution under section 776.032(1), Florida Statutes (2009), which is part of what is commonly known as the "Stand Your Ground" law. Because this issue involves a determination of whether the circuit court has continuing jurisdiction over Little, see Tsavaris v. Scruggs, 360 So.2d 745, 747 (Fla.1977), we treat the petition for writ of certiorari as a petition for writ of prohibition.1 We agree with Little that his use of deadly force was justified under the circumstances. We also reject the State's alternative argument that Little was not entitled to immunity under the Stand Your Ground law because he was engaged in an unlawful activity at the time he used the deadly force. We therefore grant Little's petition for writ of prohibition.

### I. Facts
The incident in question occurred when Little was walking to his girlfriend's house with his friend, Rashad Matthews. The two men happened upon

Matthews' friend, Terry Lester, who was standing in the driveway of his mother's home. Lester was leaning into the driver's door of a vehicle parked in the driveway when Matthews approached and engaged Lester in conversation. Little, who was a stranger to Lester, initially waited for Matthews by the street.

After a few minutes, Little started walking toward the two men. When Little reached the driver's side of the car, Demond Brooks jumped out of the back seat. Little knew Brooks, but the two were not friends. Without warning, Brooks pulled two handguns from his waistband, pointed them at Little, and yelled that he was "going to make it rain." Little believed Brooks was threatening to shoot him, so he ran behind Lester and asked Lester to intervene, or to "get" Brooks. Lester tried to calm Brooks down to no avail.

Lester's mother, Janet Speed, heard the commotion from inside the house and came to the open front door for a moment. Little used the distraction as an opportunity to obtain shelter and ran into the house. Brooks followed Little but stopped on the second of the three front porch steps. From there, Brooks held his guns down by his sides and yelled through the open door for Little to come outside. Little pressed his back up against the wall, pulled a handgun out of his pants pocket, and held it down by his side. He called to Ms. Speed to "get" Brooks.

*217 Ms. Speed had not seen Little arm himself. Ms. Speed was alerted to the gun by her daughter-in-law, Kimberly, who was also in the room. Little, who was visibly afraid, tried to explain that he was holding the gun because Brooks was threatening to shoot him from outside. Ms. Speed did not want a gun in her house and responded by telling Little to leave. But Brooks was still on the porch step yelling for Little to come outside. Little told Ms. Speed, "I ain't going out there," and said something about both men having their "fire." Ms. Speed called for her son Lester.

Lester then came into the house and ordered Little out. Little begged for Lester to stop Brooks, but Lester offered no help. In fact, Lester appeared to think the situation was funny because he had been laughing with Brooks as he passed him on his way inside the house.

Seeing no backdoor exit, Little reluctantly exited the house through the front door. Brooks backed up to let Little pass, but Brooks still had his guns down by his sides. Little proceeded cautiously, turning sideways to stay facing Brooks and keeping his gun hidden behind his back. When Little reached the yard, Brooks walked toward him and said something like, "[D]o you know what he did to me?" Little told Brooks to calm down and backed away. Brooks did not take action until Little backed into the car parked in the driveway. Then Brooks raised his guns and pointed them at Little. Little brought his gun around, closed his eyes, and pulled the trigger several times. Brooks dropped to the ground and eventually succumbed to his gunshot wounds. Little fled to his girlfriend's house.

## II. Circuit Court Proceedings

In support of his motion to dismiss, Little argued that he shot Brooks in self-defense and was therefore entitled to immunity under the Stand Your Ground law. The State raised two arguments against the motion: (1) Little was not acting in self-defense because he reengaged Brooks after removing himself from the initial threat, and (2) Little was not entitled to immunity under the Stand Your Ground law because he was engaged in an unlawful activity as a felon in possession of a firearm. The circuit court denied the motion to dismiss, ruling as follows:

The Defendant removed himself from the zone of uncertainty when he entered the home of Janet Speed. The Defendant then chose to arm himself and re-engage the decedent, Demond Brooks. The Court at this time has not considered, the issue of whether Defendant's activity of arming himself was lawful or unlawful and need not address that issue for purposes of making a legal ruling on the matter before the Court.

## III. Analysis

A. Standard of Review

In reviewing a petition for writ of prohibition, this court must consider the merits of Little's motion to dismiss in the same manner as if it were on direct appeal. See Sutton v. State, 975 So.2d 1073, 1077–78 (Fla.2008); Hair v. State, 17 So.3d 804, 805 (Fla. 1st DCA 2009), review denied, 60 So.3d 1055 (Fla.2011). Thus, we review the court's legal findings de novo and we review the court's factual findings for competent, substantial evidence. Hair, 17 So.3d at 805.

B. Propriety of the Denial of the Motion to Dismiss on the Merits

The Stand Your Ground law is codified in chapter 776, Florida Statutes (2009). Section 776.032(1) grants criminal immunity to persons using force as permitted *218 in sections 776.012, 776.013, or 776.031. In this case, Little argued he was entitled to immunity under section 776.032(1) because his use of force was permitted in section 776.012(1). Section 776.012(1) authorizes the use of deadly force when a defendant "reasonably believes that such force is necessary to prevent imminent death or great bodily harm to himself or herself." A defendant must establish entitlement to immunity under the Stand Your Ground law by a preponderance of the evidence.

Horn v. State, 17 So.3d 836, 839 (Fla. 2d DCA 2009).

In determining that Little was not entitled to immunity under the Stand Your Ground law, the circuit court concluded that Little removed himself from the imminent threat of death or great bodily harm by going into Ms. Speed's house but "chose to arm himself and re-engage" Brooks. Thus, the court determined that Little was not "in the zone of uncertainty." See Montanez v. State, 24 So.3d 799, 801–03 (Fla. 2d DCA 2010) (holding that circuit court properly denied criminal immunity to a defendant who shot the victim after the victim had driven his car at the defendant and his employee because "the zone of uncertainty" had already passed when the defendant and the employee had gotten out of the vehicle's path and there was therefore no threat of imminent death or great bodily harm).

Little argues that the circuit court's ruling is erroneous because it is not supported by competent, substantial evidence. Little acknowledges that he had removed himself from Brooks' line of fire by entering Ms. Speed's home. He argues that he did not choose to leave Ms. Speed's home but was forced to do so. He also claims that he did not reengage Brooks but made every attempt to avoid an encounter.

We agree that the circuit court's ruling is not supported by the evidence. Specifically, there is no evidence whatsoever that Little reengaged Brooks. The evidence establishes that Little was afraid of Brooks and repeatedly asked for help in calming Brooks down. While Little was able to remove himself from the imminent threat of death or great bodily harm by running inside Ms. Speed's house, Little was ordered outside by Ms. Speed herself and then her son Lester. Little did not see a backdoor exit, so he went out the way he came in. Little walked past Brooks with extreme caution and with his gun out of sight. When Brooks started ranting at him, Little implored Brooks to calm down. There is no evidence that Little made any threatening moves toward Brooks or said any threatening words to him. But Brooks raised his guns and pointed them at Little anyway, and Little responded to the threat.

Thus, the circuit court erred in concluding that Little's use of deadly force was not justified under the circumstances. However, that does not end our analysis because the State has asserted another basis on which to uphold the circuit court's ruling, or a "tipsy coachman" argument.2

C. State's Tipsy Coachman Argument
The State argues that regardless of whether Little established that his use of deadly force was permitted in section 776.012(1), he was not entitled to

immunity under section 776.032(1) because his use of force would not have been permitted in section 776.013(3). The State notes that in order for a person's use of deadly force to *219 be permitted in section 776.013(3), the person must not be engaged in an unlawful activity. Because Little was a felon in illegal possession of a firearm, the State submits that he was engaged in an unlawful activity and cannot obtain immunity under any of these statutory provisions.

Section 776.032(1) provides, in pertinent part, "A person who uses force as permitted in s. 776.012, s. 776.013, or s. 776.031 is justified in using such force and is immune from criminal prosecution and civil action for the use of such force...." Because section 776.032(1) grants criminal immunity to persons using force as permitted in section 776.012, section 776.013, or section 776.031, it should be construed to allow a defendant to claim immunity based on the use of force permitted in any of these provisions. See Pompano Horse Club v. State, 93 Fla. 415, 111 So. 801, 805 (1927) ("[T]he word 'or' is usually, if not always, construed judicially as a disjunctive unless it becomes necessary in order to conform to the clear intention of the Legislature to construe it conjunctively as meaning 'and.' ").

Despite the disjunctive language in section 776.032(1), the State asserts that the legislature did not intend to provide immunity based on the use of force as permitted in section 776.012(1) because section 776.012(1) conflicts with section 776.013(3). According to the State, both sections 776.012(1) and 776.013(3) permit the use of deadly force based on a reasonable belief such force is necessary to prevent imminent death or great bodily harm or the commission of a felony. The State argues that section 776.013(3) limits the justifiable use of deadly force to persons who are not engaged in illegal activity and who are in a place they have a legal right to be. The State asserts that section 776.012(1) cannot provide a separate basis for immunity because it would provide immunity for a person engaged in an unlawful activity and thus render section 776.013(3) meaningless. We cannot agree.

"A court's purpose in construing a statute is to give effect to legislative intent, which is the polestar that guides the court in statutory construction." Larimore v. State, 2 So.3d 101, 106 (Fla.2008). We first look to the plain language of the statute to discern legislative intent. And we must interpret the statute to give meaning to each of its provisions. Id. " 'The doctrine of in pari materia is a principle of statutory construction that requires that statutes relating to the same subject or object be construed together to harmonize the statutes and to give effect to the Legislature's intent.' " Id. (quoting Fla. Dep't of State v. Martin, 916 So.2d 763, 768 (Fla.2005)).

We conclude that the plain language of sections 776.012, 776.013, and 776.032 can be understood as granting immunity to a person who qualifies under either section 776.012(1) or 776.013(3). To arrive at this conclusion, we will examine the provisions in sections 776.012 and 776.013 in pari materia to determine whether the legislature intended for each section to provide a separate basis for immunity under section 776.032(1). Our analysis will begin with a review of the law governing the justifiable use of deadly force prior to the enactment of the Stand Your Ground law. We will then examine the effect of the enactment of the Stand Your Ground law on that body of law to discern the extent to which the legislature intended to change that law.

Prior to the enactment of the Stand Your Ground law, the justifiable use of deadly force by and against a civilian was governed by section 776.012. Section 776.012, Florida Statutes (2004), permitted the use of deadly force if a person "reasonably believes that such force is necessary *220 to prevent imminent death or great bodily harm to himself or herself or another or to prevent the imminent commission of a forcible felony." Section 776.031 governed the use of force in defense of others, and it permitted the use of deadly force if a person "reasonably believes that such force is necessary to prevent the imminent commission of a forcible felony." In addition, the Florida Supreme Court recognized a common law duty to retreat that required a person to "retreat to the wall" or use "every reasonable means within his or her power to avoid the danger." Weiand v. State, 732 So.2d 1044, 1049, 1050 (Fla.1999). There was an exception to the duty to retreat for a person claiming self-defense in his or her own residence; that exception was part of the "castle doctrine."3 Id.

In 2005, the legislature enacted the Stand Your Ground law which amended sections 776.012 and .031 and created sections 776.013 and .032. Ch. 2005–27, §§ 1–4, at 200–02, Laws of Fla. Section 776.012 still permits the justifiable use of deadly force if a person "reasonably believes that such force is necessary to prevent imminent death or great bodily harm to himself or herself or another or to prevent the imminent commission of a forcible felony." § 776.012(1). But the Stand Your Ground law added language permitting the justifiable use of deadly force "[u]nder those circumstances permitted pursuant to s. 776.013." § 776.012(2). It also eliminated the common law duty to retreat for persons justifiably using deadly force under either section 776.012(1) or 776.013.

Section 776.012, which is entitled "Use of force in defense of person," now provides as follows:

A person is justified in using force, except deadly force, against another when and to the extent that the person reasonably believes that such conduct is necessary to defend himself or herself or another against the other's imminent use of unlawful force. However, a person is justified in the use of deadly force and does not have a duty to retreat if:

(1) He or she reasonably believes that such force is necessary to prevent imminent death or great bodily harm to himself or herself or another or to prevent the imminent commission of a forcible felony; or

(2) Under those circumstances permitted pursuant to s. 776.013.

As for section 776.013, it is entitled "Home protection; use of deadly force; presumption of fear of death or great bodily harm."4 Subsections (1), (2), (4), and (5) of section 776.013 expand the "castle" to include a dwelling, residence, or occupied vehicle. These subsections all work together to provide for presumptions that make it easier for a person in the "castle" to establish the justifiable use of deadly force. Subsection (1) sets forth a presumption of "a reasonable fear of imminent peril of death or great bodily harm." § 776.013(1). Subsection (2) sets forth four circumstances in which the presumption in subsection (1) does not apply, including when "[t]he person who uses defensive force is engaged in an unlawful activity." § 776.013(2)(c). Subsection (4) *221 sets forth a presumption that "[a] person who unlawfully and by force enters or attempts to enter a person's dwelling, residence, or occupied vehicle is presumed to be doing so with the intent to commit an unlawful act involving force or violence." § 776.013(4). And subsection (5) defines "dwelling," "residence," and "vehicle." § 776.013(5).

Subsection (3), which is the subsection on which the State focuses, applies to "[a] person who is not engaged in an unlawful activity and who is attacked in any other place where he or she has a right to be." § 776.013(3). It eliminates the duty to retreat for this law-abiding person. It also provides for the use of deadly force by this law-abiding person based upon the reasonable belief "it is necessary to do so to prevent death or great bodily harm to himself or herself or another or to prevent the commission of a forcible felony." Id.

We do not agree that there is a conflict between the provisions in sections 776.012(1) and 776.013(3). Section 776.013(3) provides for the justifiable use of deadly force by a law-abiding person outside of the "castle," but it does not preclude persons who are engaged in an unlawful activity from using deadly force in self-defense when otherwise permitted. In fact, the Stand Your Ground law expressly amended section 776.012 to provide that the use of deadly force is justified under the circumstances set forth in both sections 776.012(1) and 776.013.

Nor do we agree that construing section 776.012(1) as a distinct statute permitting the justifiable use of deadly force would render section 776.013(3) meaningless. Instead, the burden of proof and the entitlement to the various presumptions to assist in meeting that burden varies depending upon which statute applies.

Section 776.013(3) applies when a person is (1) not engaged in an unlawful activity and (2) attacked in any place outside the "castle" as long as (3) he or she has a right to be there. A person who does not meet these three requirements would look to section 776.012(1) to determine whether the use of deadly force was justified. The presumptions in sections 776.013(1) and (4) apply only when a person is attacked in the "castle." And the presumption in section 776.013(1) does not apply if the person was engaged in an unlawful activity. See § 776.013(2)(c).

The requirements under sections 776.012(1) and 776.013(3) are not identical. A person proceeding under section 776.013(3) would have to prove that he or she reasonably believed the use of deadly force was "necessary ... to prevent death or great bodily harm ... or to prevent the commission of a forcible felony." Under section 776.012(1), a person would have to prove that he or she reasonably believed the use of deadly force was "necessary to prevent imminent death or great bodily harm ... or to prevent the imminent commission of a forcible felony." (Emphasis added.)

As for criminal immunity, a person engaged in an unlawful activity would not be entitled to claim immunity under section 776.032(1) based on the use of force as permitted in section 776.013(3). But section 776.013(3) provides only one means of obtaining immunity under section 776.032(1). Section 776.012(1) provides another means of obtaining immunity for individuals who would not qualify for immunity under section 776.013(3). And section 776.032(1) expressly provides for immunity based on the use of force as permitted in section 776.012.

In summary, section 776.032(1) provides for immunity from criminal prosecution for persons using force as permitted in section 776.012, section 776.013, or *222 section 776.031. Because Little was a felon in illegal possession of a firearm, his use of force did not fall within the protections of section 776.013, and therefore, he could not obtain immunity under that statute. See Darling v. State, 81 So.3d 574, 578 (Fla. 3d DCA 2012), review denied, 107 So.3d 403 (Fla.2012); Dorsey v. State, 74 So.3d 521, 527 (Fla. 4th DCA 2011). However, Little sought immunity based on the use of force as permitted in section 776.012(1). His status as a felon in illegal possession of a firearm did not preclude that claim of immunity. And, as set forth above, Little established by a preponderance of the evidence that his use of force was justified to prevent his imminent death or great bodily harm as provided for in section 776.012(1). Accordingly, Little was entitled to immunity under section 776.032(1).

The parties have not cited and we have not located any cases addressing the specific issue presented here. However, we have considered, among other cases, the Fourth District's decision in State v. Hill, 95 So.3d 434 (Fla. 4th DCA 2012). In Hill, the defendant was charged with aggravated battery with a firearm, possession of a firearm by a convicted felon, and other crimes after he shot a man in the stomach during an altercation over a woman. Id. at 434–35. The defendant filed a motion to dismiss the aggravated battery charge in which he argued that he was entitled to immunity under the Stand Your Ground law based on the justifiable use of force. Id. at 434. He claimed that he was attacked by two men, one of whom had a gun, while sitting on his own porch and that he could not retreat because he was cornered. Id. at 434–35.

The circuit court granted the defendant's motion to dismiss and rejected the argument that the defendant was precluded from seeking immunity under the Stand Your Ground law because he was engaged in an unlawful activity as a felon in illegal possession of a firearm. Id. at 435. The Fourth District reversed. Id. at 435. The court concluded that the crime of possession of a firearm by a convicted felon qualified as unlawful activity under section 776.013(3). And the court explained that under section 776.013(3) the defendant was not entitled to immunity because he was engaged in an unlawful activity. Id.

The Fourth District has not addressed whether a defendant would be entitled to immunity based on the use of force as permitted in section 776.012(1). As we have already explained, section 776.032(1) provides for immunity based on the use of force as permitted in three separate statutory provisions: section 776.012, section 776.013, or section 776.031. As pertains to the circumstances here, even though Little's use of force was not permitted in section 776.013(3), it was permitted in section 776.012(1).

D. Certification of Conflict and Question for Resolution by Supreme Court
To the extent that the Fourth District's decision in Hill can be read as holding that a defendant who is engaged in an unlawful activity is not entitled to immunity under section 776.032(1), we certify conflict. Additionally, we recognize the significance of a determination of whether a defendant is entitled to criminal immunity as well as the ever-increasing

attempts to invoke that immunity by persons charged with serious crimes. We therefore certify the following question as one of great public importance:

IS A DEFENDANT WHO ESTABLISHES BY A PREPONDERANCE OF THE EVIDENCE THAT HIS USE OF DEADLY FORCE IS PERMITTED IN SECTION 776.012(1), FLORIDA STATUTES (2009), ENTITLED TO *223 IMMUNITY UNDER SECTION 776.032(1) EVEN THOUGH HE IS ENGAGED IN AN UNLAWFUL ACTIVITY AT THE TIME HE USES THE DEADLY FORCE?

Petition granted.

VILLANTI, J., Concurs.
NORTHCUTT, J. Concurs with opinion.
NORTHCUTT, Judge, Concurring.

. . . .

---

## Mobley v. State, 132 So.3d 1160 (Fla. 3rd DCA, 2014)

Petition granted.

Salter, J., filed a dissenting opinion.

Before SHEPHERD, C.J., and WELLS and SALTER, JJ.

### Opinion

WELLS, Judge.

We have jurisdiction to review the instant petition for writ of prohibition seeking to preclude the court below from proceeding further in adjudicating criminal charges against petitioner, Gabriel Mobley, on the grounds that Mobley is immune from prosecution under the provisions of Chapter 776 of the Florida Statutes (Florida's Stand Your Ground Law). See Mederos v. State, 102 So.3d 7, 11 (Fla. 1st DCA 2012) ("A writ of prohibition is the proper vehicle for challenging a trial court's denial of a motion to dismiss a charge on the ground of immunity from prosecution pursuant to the Stand Your Ground Law."); see also Little v. State, 111 So.3d 214, 216 n. 1 (Fla. 2d DCA 2013) ("We believe that the better avenue for review [of orders denying motions to dismiss asserting immunity under the Stand Your Ground Law] is a petition for writ of prohibition, which the supreme court has consistently held is an appropriate vehicle to review orders denying motions to dismiss in criminal prosecutions based on immunity.").

The standard of review applicable to this case is the same as that which is applied to the denial of a motion to suppress. See Mederos, 102 So.3d at 11 (stating that "a review of a trial court's order on a motion claiming immunity under the [Stand Your Ground] statute is governed by the same standard which applies in an appeal from an order denying a motion to suppress"); State v. Vino, 100 So.3d 716 (Fla. 3d DCA 2012) (citing Mederos for the *1162 applicable standard of review). Under this standard, the trial court's findings of fact are "presumed correct and can be reversed only if they are not supported by competent substantial evidence," while the trial court's legal conclusions are reviewed de novo. Vino, 100 So.3d at 719. For the reasons that follow, we grant the petition but withhold issuance of our writ confident that the court below will comply with this court's order.

## Facts

Gabriel Mobley, the petitioner here, was charged with two counts of second degree murder following a shooting which took place outside a local Chili's restaurant on February 27, 2008. The day of the fatal shooting, Mobley finished work around 3:00 pm at his pressure cleaning business, and after going home to shower and change, went to work at the tax preparation office of high school friend, Jose (Chico) Correa.1 After working several hours at Chico's business, Mobley was invited by Chico to join him and his staff at a local Chili's to unwind. Mobley agreed to join them but drove his own car intending to go home from the restaurant. When Mobley arrived at the restaurant, he removed the handgun that he was carrying and stowed the gun in the glove compartment of his car.2 He did so because he believed from the training that he had received to secure a concealed carry license that firearms could not be brought into any establishment where food and alcohol are served.3 By the time Mobley got to the restaurant, a number of Chico's female employees had arrived and were sitting at a booth located near one end of the restaurant's bar. Because the booth was crowded, Mobley, Chico, and another of Chico's employees (another man) sat at the bar nearest the booth.

Sometime after food and drinks were ordered, Mobley and Chico went outside to smoke. They returned to the bar where they ate, drank and conversed without incident. However, things changed after Mobley and

Chico went outside a second time for a smoke. This time when they reentered the restaurant, they found two men, later identified as Jason Gonzalez and Rolando (Roly) Carrazana, talking to Chico's female employees. According to Chico, the women seemed to be uncomfortable so he told the men to leave. This sparked a verbal altercation between Chico and the two men which continued until the two men returned to their table at the other end of the bar. The altercation, which lasted only a few minutes, was loud enough to attract the attention of the restaurant's security guard and its manager, who asked the guard to keep an eye on Jason and Roly.

Mobley was not involved in the argument but acted as peacemaker instead, going to Jason's and Roly's table to ask them to forget what he described as a petty misunderstanding. He even shook Jason's hand and gave him a friendly pat on the back. Mobley also spoke to a third person seated at the bar who appeared to be with Jason and Roly about forgetting *1163 this petty disagreement.4

Although the altercation appeared to have ended, Mobley testified that he began to feel uncomfortable after he noticed Roly staring in the direction of Chico's party with a "mean, cold [look] on his face."5 He decided it was time to leave. But before he left, he and Chico went to the restroom where he expressed his concerns to his friend. As Mobley and Chico were returning from the bathroom, they passed the front of the restaurant where Mobley saw Jason, with Roly nearby, banging aggressively on the restaurant's window and pointing toward them.6 When Mobley and Chico reached their seats, Mobley suggested that after Jason and Roly left, they should all go home. Approximately ten to fifteen minutes later, after Jason and Roly appeared to have left, Mobley left the restaurant alone while Chico settled the check.

The events that transpired next were captured on a security camera recording made outside the restaurant, and, for the most part, are beyond dispute. The recording shows that at 23:52:15, Mobley, wearing only a sleeveless tee shirt, exited the Chili's front door and went to his vehicle parked only feet away, but mostly outside the security camera's viewing range. There, Mobley, as subsequent footage confirms, donned a sweat shirt, because, according to Mobley, it was chilly that night.7 He also retrieved his gun and put it in a holster that he wore around his waist. Less than a minute after Mobley left the restaurant, Chico and the third man in their party exited the front door. Chico was joined by Mobley who walked with Chico to his nearby car.8 There the two remained for approximately thirty seconds until, at 23:53:38, Mobley stepped onto the sidewalk near the front fender of Chico's car. Approximately twenty seconds later, Chico joined him on the sidewalk where the two smoked a cigarette.

Four seconds after Chico joined Mobley on the sidewalk, Jason Gonzalez can be seen rapidly approaching from Mobley's and Chico's right. Four seconds after that, Jason delivered a vicious punch to Chico's face which fractured Chico's eye socket. Jason then can be seen to dance backward, hands raised in a fighter's pose, and within four seconds of landing the punch on Chico advance forward toward Mobley. Mobley reacted by raising his arm and hand to ward Jason off. Two seconds later, as Jason steps back from Mobley, Roly can be seen rushing up from the rear of the restaurant to join Jason in what Mobley testified he believed to be a renewed attack on both himself and Chico. At this juncture, as Roly neared Jason, who was only feet from both Mobley and Chico, Mobley testified that he saw Roly reach under his long, baggy shirt. Believing that Roly was reaching for a weapon to *1164 use in an attack, Mobley drew his gun and shot at Roly hitting both Roly and Jason.

This entire series of events, from the time Jason first comes into view on the sidewalk until the first shot was fired, took only twelve seconds. After being shot, Jason turned and fled toward his (or Roly's) car to collapse with a gunshot wound to the chest and die. Roly, hit four times, fell to the ground near the restaurant's door where he was assisted by the third man in their party who had been sitting at the bar. Roly later died at a local hospital. Although no weapons were found on Roly's body, two knives were found on the ground near where he fell.9

Following the shooting, Mobley remained at the scene and had the other members of his party, who by then were leaving in their cars, return to wait for the authorities. When police officers arrived only minutes later, Mobley told them that he was armed and otherwise fully cooperated with them. After being held in a police car for a number of hours, he was transported to the police station where he was read and waived his Miranda10 rights. While there, he gave both an unsworn and a sworn statement. He was then released but not charged.

Several weeks later, after a new lead investigator had been assigned to the case, Mobley agreed to be and was re-interviewed. While there is no indication that his version of the events changed in any manner during this interview, he subsequently was arrested and charged with two counts of second degree murder. Mobley claimed below and now claims here that these facts are undisputed and demonstrate that he is immune from prosecution as provided by sections 776.012 and 776.032 of the Florida

Statutes. We agree in part that the pertinent facts are not in dispute and that Mobley is entitled to immunity from prosecution.

## Analysis

Florida law confers immunity from criminal prosecution and civil liability, without the obligation to retreat, on those who use deadly force reasonably believing that the use of such force is necessary to either prevent imminent death or great bodily harm to self or others or to prevent the imminent commission of a forcible felony. See § 776.032, Fla. Stat. (2013) (providing that a "person who uses force as permitted in s. 776.012, s. 776.013, or s. 776.031 is justified in using such force and is immune from criminal prosecution and civil action for the use of such force"); see also § 776.012(1), (2), Fla. Stat. (2013) (providing that a "person is justified in the use of deadly force ... and does not have a duty to retreat if: (1) [h]e or she reasonably believes that such force is necessary to prevent imminent death or great bodily harm to himself or herself or another or to prevent the imminent commission of a forcible felony; or (2) [u]nder those circumstances permitted pursuant to s. 776.013").

An objective standard is applied to determine whether the immunity provided by these provisions attaches. See Montanez v. State, 24 So.3d 799, 803 (Fla. 2d DCA 2010) (confirming that in determining whether the immunity accorded by section 776.032 attaches, "the objective, reasonable person standard by which claims of justifiable use of deadly force are measured" should be applied). That standard requires the court to determine whether, based on circumstances as they appeared to the defendant when he or she acted, a *1165 reasonable and prudent person situated in the same circumstances and knowing what the defendant knew would have used the same force as did the defendant. See Toledo v. State, 452 So.2d 661, 663 (Fla. 3d DCA 1984) ("[A] person in the exercise of his right of self-defense may use 'only such force as a reasonable person, situated as he was and knowing what he knew, would have used under like circumstances.' " (quoting People v. Moody, 62 Cal.App.2d 18, 143 P.2d 978, 980 (1943))); see also Chaffin v. State, 121 So.3d 608 (Fla. 4th DCA 2013) (confirming that the standard to be applied for determining whether a person is justified in using deadly force in self-defense is not a subjective standard as to the defendant's state of mind, but an objective standard as to a reasonably prudent person's state of mind); Price v. Gray's Guard Service, Inc., 298 So.2d 461, 464 (Fla. 1st DCA 1974) ("The conduct of a person acting in self defense is measured by an objective standard, but the standard must be applied to the facts and circumstances as they appeared at the time of the altercation to the one acting in self defense.").

Here, the court below determined that Mobley did not "reasonably" believe that deadly force was "necessary" to prevent "imminent" death, great bodily harm, or commission of a forcible felony. In doing so, the court discounted the totality of the circumstances facing Mobley and concluded that the use of deadly force was not reasonable, first, because Mobley "never saw a weapon and did not know anything about the possibility of a weapon," with him only seeing "the second attacker appear to be reaching for something under his shirt," and second, because Mobley should have brandished his gun, fired a warning shot or told the attackers to stop because he had a gun. We disagree for the following reasons.

As a preliminary matter, Mobley was not required to warn that he had a gun. Section 776.012(1), (2), clearly states where the danger of death, great bodily harm or the commission of a forcible felony is "imminent," the use of deadly force is justified. The statute contains no warning requirement. See T.P. v. State, 117 So.3d 864, 866 (Fla. 4th DCA 2013) (quoting McWhorter v. State, 971 So.2d 154, 156 (Fla. 4th DCA 2007)) ("... [U]nder section 776.013, a person who is attacked is allowed to stand his or her ground and 'meet force with force.' It appears that the new law places no duty on the person to avoid or retreat from danger, so long as that person is not engaged in an unlawful activity and is located in a place where he or she has a right to be. § 776.013(3), Fla. Stat. (2005) (Internal citation omitted).").

As to the primary reason given by the court for rejecting Mobley's "Stand Your Ground" defense—that Mobley did not see a weapon, this likewise cannot be deemed determinative. The record reflects that Mobley observed Jason viciously attack his friend Chico outside the Chili's. Mobley then saw Jason's friend Roly approach and reach under his shirt. It was then that Mobley became afraid for his safety and life and for that of his friend and he pulled his gun:

Q. Okay. So, as soon as he [Roly] was coming towards you, you shot?
A. Yes.
Q. Why did you first pull your firearm?
A. Why[?]
Q. Yes.
A. By this time, you know, I didn't know what they had done—I didn't know what Chico had got hit with, and it was so much blood, I freaked, I was scared and I seen [sic] this other guy coming up from the back.

*1166 And he reached up under his shirt. So, I was scared, I thought, they were going to shoot or kill us or stab us or something. So I was scared.

The shooting at issue did not occur in a vacuum. Mobley did not shoot two innocent bystanders who just happened upon him on a sidewalk. The record—as corroborated by a video of the events—is that (1) Mobley found himself in the middle of a violent, unprovoked attack on a companion who was standing right next to him, by one of two men who earlier had engaged in an altercation to which he was a witness; (2) after the initial violent attack on Mobley's friend, the attacker immediately turned his attention to Mobley; (3) less than four seconds after that, the first attacker was joined by the second man involved in the altercation inside the restaurant; and (4) when the second man reached under his shirt after rushing up to join his companion who had not abandoned the field, Mobley believed the second man was reaching for a weapon to continue the attack. With these facts at hand, and with Mobley's knowledge of these two assailants, the issue for determination was not whether Mobley knew a weapon was possible or whether he actually saw one, but whether a reasonably prudent person in those same circumstances and with the same knowledge would have used the force Mobley used.

Rather than applying the objective standard required, the court below instead focused on the events that transpired inside the Chili's to entirely discount Mobley's "expressed beliefs or intentions" about what occurred outside the Chili's. The court found that because Mobley was not directly involved in the earlier altercation inside the restaurant between Chico and Jason/Roly, but had acted as peacemaker, he could not have feared for his own life during the events which happened later outside the restaurant. However the events that occurred inside the Chili's are relevant only insofar as they provide the context for Mobley's actions when the attack outside the restaurant occurred.

It may have been more prudent for Mobley and Chico to skitter to their cars and hightail it out of there when they had the chance; however, as even the State concedes and the court below recognized, Mobley and Chico had every right to be where they were, doing what they were doing and they did nothing to precipitate this violent attack. The only relevant inquiry was whether, given the totality of the circumstances leading up to the attack, the appearance of danger was so real that a reasonably cautious and prudent person under the same circumstances would have believed that the danger could be avoided only through the use of deadly force.

Because the preponderance of the evidence demonstrates that had the proper standard been applied, Mobley's use of deadly force was justified, the motion to dismiss should have been granted. See Dennis v. State, 51

So.3d 456, 460 (Fla.2010) (confirming that, where a defendant claims immunity from prosecution under sections 776.012, 776.013 and 776.032, the court below must determine whether that defendant has shown by a preponderance of the evidence that the immunity attaches); Vino, 100 So.3d at 717 ("When a defendant invokes the statutory immunity, the trial court must hold a pre-trial evidentiary hearing to determine if the preponderance of the evidence warrants immunity.").

In so holding, we are mindful that, under our standard of review which is akin to that applied to the trial court's ruling on a motion to suppress, the trial court's ruling comes to this court "clothed with a presumption of correctness and the court must interpret the evidence and reasonable *1167 inferences and deductions derived therefrom in a manner most favorable to sustaining the trial court's ruling." See R.J.C. v. State, 84 So.3d 1250, 1254 (Fla. 4th DCA 2012) (quoting Terry v. State, 668 So.2d 954, 958 (Fla.1996)); Smith v. State, 719 So.3d 1018, 1021 (Fla. 3d DCA 1998) (same). Nevertheless, considering the entire record and reasonable inferences derived therefrom in a manner most favorable to the trial court's ruling, we nonetheless find there is no basis to support the trial court's decision to deny immunity in this case.

Petition granted.

SHEPHERD, C.J., concurs.
SALTER, J. (dissenting).

. . . .

Made in the USA
Coppell, TX
12 November 2021